Cambridge Elements

Elements in Data Rights and Wrongs
edited by
Damian Clifford
London School of Economics
Jeannie Marie Paterson
University of Melbourne

AI MENTAL HEALTH SUPPORT AND THE CASE FOR DISTRIBUTED NETWORKED REGULATION

Jeannie Marie Paterson
The University of Melbourne

CAMBRIDGE
UNIVERSITY PRESS

CAMBRIDGE
UNIVERSITY PRESS

Shaftesbury Road, Cambridge CB2 8EA, United Kingdom

One Liberty Plaza, 20th Floor, New York, NY 10006, USA

477 Williamstown Road, Port Melbourne, VIC 3207, Australia

314–321, 3rd Floor, Plot 3, Splendor Forum, Jasola District Centre, New Delhi – 110025, India

Cambridge University Press is part of Cambridge University Press & Assessment, a department of the University of Cambridge.

We share the University's mission to contribute to society through the pursuit of education, learning and research at the highest international levels of excellence.

www.cambridge.org
Information on this title: www.cambridge.org/9781009860772
DOI: 10.1017/9781009860796

When citing this work, please include a reference to the DOI 10.1017/9781009860796

First published 2026

A catalogue record for this publication is available from the British Library

A Cataloging-in-Publication data record for this Element is available from the Library of Congress

ISBN 978-1-009-86081-9 Hardback
ISBN 978-1-009-86077-2 Paperback
ISSN 2976-7520 (online)
ISSN 2976-7512 (print)

AI Mental Health Support and the Case for Distributed Networked Regulation

Elements in Data Rights and Wrongs

DOI: 10.1017/9781009860796
First published online: July 2026

Jeannie Marie Paterson
The University of Melbourne

Author for correspondence: Jeannie Marie Paterson, jeanniep@unimelb.edu.au

Abstract: Clinicians and consumers have long been interested in using purpose-built chatbots to provide mental health support. Specifically designed 'therapy bots' are now available direct-to-consumer, even though researchers have yet to establish their efficacy, safety and viability. Whatever their merits or limitations, the role for specialised therapy bots has been overshadowed by the increasing number of people using AI companions and general-purpose generative AI chatbots for mental health support. Reports have implicated these offerings in instances of user self-harm and psychosis, prompting calls for more robust regulation across the entire field. This Element examines the opportunities, risks and legal landscape of AI for direct-to-consumer therapy bots and related digital mental health support tools and considers a response of distributed regulatory networks. This approach abandons any pretence of a single body of law providing an effective and palatable response to concerns raised by therapy bots and the challenges posed by evolving technologies operating in sensitive domains.

Keywords: AI mental health, therapy bot, generative AI, chatbot, companion AI, consumer protection, data protection, medical product safety

ISBNs: 9781009860819 (HB), 9781009860772 (PB), 9781009860796 (OC)
ISSNs: 2976-7520 (online), 2976-7512 (print)

Contents

Introduction

Increasingly sophisticated generative AI chatbots are moving into one of the most sensitive areas of healthcare: mental health support. Consumers seeking to improve their mental health or well-being may now seek assistance from a multitude of online 'therapy bots' and related digital tools specifically designed to provide mental health or well-being support without the intervention of a human health professional. Consumers may also choose to interact with online services that do not specifically offer this expertise, but appear capable of providing it, including through AI companions and general-purpose generative AI chatbots. The use of AI for therapy has a historical precursor. Eliza, an early chatbot, was developed in 1966 by MIT computer scientist Joseph Weizenbaum to demonstrate the possibility of human–machine conversation (Weizenbaum, 1976). The Eliza chatbot used a Rogerian psychotherapy technique, reframing users' statements as questions (Weizenbaum, 1976: 3). For some, these human–machine interactions illustrated the potential for machine therapists, a potential now being revisited. Others were not so sure. Weizenbaum himself warned against such uses, arguing that Eliza's seemingly natural conversational ability would lead people to attribute non-existent powers of judgment to it. Weizenbaum also argued that there were certain things a chatbot ought not to do (1976: 269–270; Tarnoff, 2023), to which lawyers might add: at least not without regulation.

Renewed interest in therapy bots has been driven by a combination of factors, including a lack of accessible mental health support, the ability to deliver services directly to consumers via smartphone or computer, the language capabilities of generative AI and a general drive to automation. These factors mean that consumers can directly access a range of digital tools designed to provide mental health or well-being support through mindfulness exercises, symptom tracking and cognitive behavioural therapy. Yet, despite significant interest and investment, the merits of therapy via AI remain uncertain. Therapy bots and related digital mental health support tools are made available without the involvement of a mental health professional, who might otherwise guide consumers on appropriate use, and the value of the use, especially without such oversight, is uncertain. The developers of therapy bots and other direct-to-consumer digital mental health support tools often claim a 'scientific' basis for their products that randomised clinical trials have not comprehensively established. To some extent, this reflects the reality that clinical trials take time and may be outpaced by the rapidly evolving technology. In any event, direct-to-consumer mental health support tools often fall outside therapeutic goods regulation and the oversight this regime exercises over medical devices. Nonetheless, therapy bots and other direct-to-consumer mental health support tools raise other kinds of risks, including breaches of confidentiality, erosion of privacy, low levels of accuracy, and bias against users who already experience unequal access to resources. Like any consumer product, the services of therapy bots risk being over-promoted by misleading marketing and undermined by overreaching exclusion and limitation clauses.

Whatever their therapeutic merits, the market for specifically designed therapy bots is being challenged by other AI-informed offerings. Recent studies suggest that consumers are seeking mental health support in AI companions, which are chatbots marketed to provide friendship, romance or companionship through avatars of attractive humans, fantasy figures or anime characters. Further, consumers are using general-purpose generative AI chatbots, such as ChatGPT, Gemini, Grok or Claude, to provide personalised mental health support and advice, bypassing completely the more specialised options. Unlike the tools designed for mental health support, AI companions and general-purpose generative AI chatbots do not purport to provide established clinical or mindfulness support. They do not claim, and often explicitly disclaim, mental health expertise, although they may make suggestions about such matters. Instead, they are trained to prolong conversation by engaging and pleasing the user (Gilbert, 2025). This combination of a lack of expertise and a tendency to sycophancy (Cheng, 2026b) may have adverse health consequences in the longer term. Notably, AI companions and general-purpose generative AI have been linked to instances of self-harm and suicide by providing inappropriate responses to users or even actively encouraging such conduct (Duffy, 2025).

Any effective response to concerns about AI used in mental health must come from the co-ordinated efforts of mental health professionals, technologists and people with lived experience. Law may also play a role. Until recently, digital tools offering mental health support, whether as a dedicated service or as part of a more general offering, have not attracted any sustained attention by relevant regulators. As with Eliza, therapy bots have been seen as largely innocuous and potentially helpful. They have not been subject to regulatory scrutiny, leaving the possibility of cumulative harms unaddressed. That position is changing. The role of AI companions and general-purpose generative AI chatbots in multiple tragic suicide cases has drawn attention to the entire sector (Hall, 2025b;

De Freitas & Cohen, 2025). Calls are growing for new laws to regulate AI chatbots that specifically or incidentally address mental health as part of their service (American Psychological Association, 2025). However, identifying an effective regulatory response is not straightforward.

One difficulty is that direct-to-consumer therapy bots and related digital mental health support tools span several legal categories: therapeutic goods, AI, online safety, data protection and consumer protection. Critical commentary has tended to address the issues of concern that arise in one category, such as privacy or therapeutic effect, without galvanising a whole-of-sector response (Wheeler, 2025). The growing use of AI companions and general-purpose generative AI chatbots for mental health support further complicates the regulatory response. Protecting consumers from general-purpose generative AI chatbots providing inappropriate advice in a field in which they do not claim expertise is very different from demanding clinical validation of digital tools specifically designed for mental health support. Moreover, while the design and purposes of the various offerings differ, they may be poorly distinguished from the consumer's perspective. Consumers may not be concerned with the credentials of an AI-informed service provided it appears to work for them. This means interventions that are well targeted in isolation may fail to improve the overall landscape of AI used for mental health support, either because they do not address the full range of risks or because they fail to engage with consumers' own experiences.

These varied considerations mean that no one legal (or policy) intervention is likely to provide an effective response to the many concerns about the risks of direct-to-consumer therapy bots or address the use of AI companions and generative AI chatbots for mental health support. Considering separately the different kinds of laws that might apply to therapy bots or companion AI will fail to address the full suite of integrated concerns. Yet even put together, it seems unlikely these various laws can be connected in a cohesive linear strategy. A different perspective is needed.

This Element suggests that a more effective approach to responding to concerns about direct-to-consumer mental health support tools, and the less specialised alternatives, lies in conceiving the relevant laws and regulators as a 'regulatory network' operating across the domain. A network perspective on regulation also means recognising other actors and institutions, such as mental health professionals, representative bodies and consumers, as part of that regulatory network (Drahos & Krygier, 2016). These stakeholders also influence the operation and understanding of digital mental health tools and the other available options for mental health support. The approach further means treating the relevant laws and responsible regulators not merely as a network but as a distributed network, in which different regulatory 'nodes' may respond to different kinds of risk at different points in time. This perspective enables an agile response to the affordances of therapy bots and other direct-to-consumer digital mental health support tools, rather than a one-size-fits-all approach to risks of harm.

In this regard, the challenges of developing an effective legal response to the opportunities and risks of direct-to-consumer therapy bots and related digital mental health support tools reflect the wider debate about how to regulate AI. It suggests that the AI debate should not focus exclusively on laws directed specifically at the technology. Nor should it become preoccupied with trying to shape existing laws to this new field of concern. Rather, tracing the interactions between laws, actors and institutions is necessary to ensure a coherent and effective response to concerns about this now largely ubiquitous technology. Implementing adequate legal safeguards around AI-informed tools also creates space to consider the social implications and limits of their use as matters of policy and values, without being distracted by the reactive need to address the immediate harms the tools may carry.

In the following discussion, Section 1 outlines the kinds of direct-to-consumer digital mental health support tools on offer and notes the key features of AI companions and general-purpose generative AI chatbots that might be used for mental health support. Section 2 examines the technology relevant to these domains. Section 3 examines the risks arising from therapy bots and related mental health support tools and the laws that address them. Section 4 brings these themes together to examine the impact of regulatory silos and the contrasting framework of distributed regulatory networks.

The analysis focuses on four key categories or 'lenses' of risk and response: therapeutic benefit, data protection, responsible AI principles and consumer protection. These categories have been chosen on the basis of their relevance to the question of how to regulate direct-to-consumer therapy bots and digital mental health support tools. Uncertain therapeutic benefit is often raised as a concern in analyses of these products, as are confidentiality and data privacy. Ethical or responsible AI considerations are increasingly considered important governance touchpoints in any AI deployment, especially where they are aimed at the public. Consumer protection matters are considered on the basis that the services of therapy bots are sold as consumer products and hence should meet the standards of safety and fairness expected in that domain.

In this analysis, the main focus is direct-to-consumer mental health support tools, especially therapy bots. Companion AI and general-purpose generative AI chatbots are considered in so far as they are being used for mental health support, but the wider concerns about these offerings, such as misinformation and their particular risks for children, are not discussed. As the Element is primarily about legal regulation, its treatment of mental health, therapeutic benefit and technology informing the relevant tools is necessarily descriptive rather than clinical.

1 Therapy Bots: An Overview

Consumers today have a wide-ranging choice of digital tools promoted directly to them for the explicit purpose of improving well-being or reducing symptoms of poor mental health, such as anxiety or sleeplessness. Consumers can also purchase AI companion services that, in offering 'friendship' or even romantic attachment, implicitly promise to reduce loneliness, a known precursor to poor mental health. General-purpose generative AI chatbots, which generate text or image outputs in response to users' prompts, present another readily available and apparently insightful source of mental health support and advice. This Section explores the reasons underlying demand for digital mental health support, the services being offered and the technologies informing those services.

1.1 Reasons for the Interest

The proliferation of direct-to-consumer therapy bots – and the use of AI companions and general-purpose generative AI chatbots for mental health support – is not entirely surprising given the unmet demand for traditional mental health services in many countries. Considerable investment in and use of online options for consumers seeking support underlines this unmet need and the urgency of attention being given to the growing domain of digital mental health support.

1.1.1 Unmet Demand

Deloitte reports that the COVID-19 pandemic exacerbated mental health concerns and triggered declines in well-being, with a dramatic rise in the prevalence of depression, anxiety, post-traumatic stress symptoms and stress (Aiyer et al., 2021; Clark & Boulos, 2022: 8). The World Economic Forum estimates that over 970 million people worldwide live with a mental illness (Klopper, 2025), while the World Health Organisation estimates more than one billion people worldwide live with a mental health condition

(World Health Organisation, 2025: vii). Accessing professional mental health support is often difficult, slow and costly (Heaney, 2025; Hickie, 2023; Stringer, 2023), for example, only one in ten people with depression worldwide receive adequate treatment (World Health Organisation, 2025: viii). The economic costs of poor mental health are predicted to exceed $16 trillion by 2030 (Klopper, 2025). The issue is particularly acute for young people: the prevalence and impact of poor mental health are increasing at an alarming rate, yet only a small proportion of young people receive appropriate care (McGorry et al., 2024).

In this context, the appeal of developing chatbots and related digital tools for mental health support is clear (World Economic Forum and Deloitte, 2021). Since the advent of the mobile phone (Flore, 2023: 33), digital mental health interventions have expanded in both voluntary and coercive settings (Bossewitch et al., 2022; Gooding, 2019). In voluntary settings, direct-to-consumer digital mental health support tools operate in different ways. Some link consumers with a mental health professional (e.g., 7 Cups; BetterHelp), while others are designed for use within a professional mental health counselling service (e.g., SilverCloud; Thrive). Others support diagnosis and treatment advice by mental health professionals, such as through experiments in digital phenotyping (Tekin, 2021: 450). Finally, and the focus of this Element, specifically designed therapy bots provide mental health support directly to consumers, while the more general offerings, AI companions and generative AI chatbots, may also be used by consumers for mental health support.

1.1.2 Growing Investment and Use

The numbers involved in the direct-to-consumer digital mental health support market are not trivial. In 2021, the American Psychological Association calculated that app stores offered 10,000 to 20,000 products expressly purporting to provide mental health support (The Economist, 2021; World Economic Forum and Deloitte, 2021: 5). In 2025, Deloitte observed that $10 billion had been invested in innovative mental health and well-being companies since 2020 (Gates, 2025).

The figures for AI companions are also impressive. In 2025, there were 337 active for-profit AI companion apps worldwide, which had been predicted to generate over $120 million by the end of that year (Perez, 2025). Use of these products is rising. The Economist reports a 2025 survey finding that 42% of high school students had interacted with, or had a friend who had interacted with, an AI as a friend, and 18% as a romantic companion (Economist, 2025a). Character.AI alone is reported to have 20 million active users in 2025 (Economist, 2025a).

Consumers are also seeking mental health support from general-purpose generative AI chatbots, such as ChatGPT, Gemini or Claude. A 2025 study reported that 13.1% of a representative sample of young adults in the United States used general-purpose AI chatbots for mental health advice (McBain et al., 2025). Increased reliance on chatbots for mental health support among young people has also been reported in the United Kingdom (Hall, 2025a) and Australia (Cross et al., 2024).

Whether due to their greater conversational engagement or their less demanding approach to mental health, general-purpose generative AI chatbots and companion AI may be outpacing purpose-built therapy bots and other direct-to-consumer digital mental health support tools in delivering mental health support. The Economist reports that

> 25% of survey respondents had used AI for therapy or would consider doing so. Of those who had turned to AI for therapy, 74% had used ChatGPT, while 21% had used Gemini; 30% had used Meta AI, Grok, Character.AI, or another general-purpose chatbot. Just 12% had used an AI tool specifically designed for mental health work (Economist, 2025b).

Although these various products differ in the support they offer to provide for well-being or good mental health, as the next Section discusses, the underlying technologies are likely similar, albeit with varying guardrails.

1.2 The Services Being Offered

As Figure 1 indicates, the service provided by tools designed specifically for digital mental health sits very close to the use that may be made of less specialised offerings, namely: companion AI and general-purpose generative AI chatbots (Figure 1).

The following Sections describe in more detail the services provided by direct-to-consumer mental health support services, as well as the service offered by companion AI and general-purpose generative AI chatbots relevant to mental health support.

1.2.1 Digital Tools Specifically Designed for Mental Health Support

Digital mental health support tools use web and app-based interfaces – including recommendations, dashboards and, increasingly, chatbots – to provide services relevant to mental health support. Some of the popular

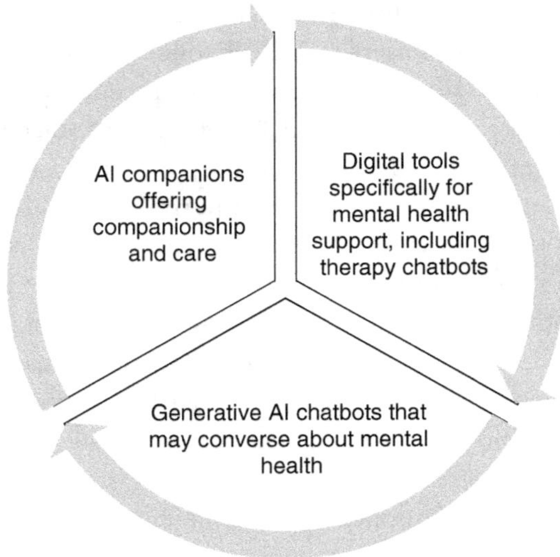

Figure 1 Kinds of services being offered

or commonly discussed direct-to-consumer mental health support tools and their self-described service are listed in Table 1.

As the descriptions in Table 1 show, it is not always clearly apparent what kind of service a direct-to-consumer mental health support tool provides. A review of popular tools available on the market suggests that they offer three main categories of service: mindfulness recommendations, mood tracking and, increasingly, therapy bots.

Mindfulness and meditation recommender tools provide curated recordings, videos and written content to support consumers in these practices. The tools may seem only loosely connected to mental health support. However, developers promote the close relationship between mindfulness and mental health, primarily in their capacity for reducing symptoms of poor mental health, such as anxiety or sleeplessness, with meditations, mindfulness techniques and general lifestyle advice.

Mood tracking tools allow consumers to record their experiences of mental health and then provide dashboards and other visualisations to assist them in tracking those symptoms. Mood tracking may be combined with monitoring physical health, notably, a service offered through the Apple Health app. Mood tracking and recommender tools, although tailored to the customer, are essentially static tools, providing resources with little interaction with the user, leading to interest in chatbots for mental health support.

Table 1 The services provided and as described by the developers of direct-to-consumer digital mental health tools

Name	Service	Marketing description used to promote the product
Calm	*Meditation and mindfulness recommendations*	'Our goal is to help you improve your health and happiness' (Calm)
Headspace	*Meditation and mindfulness recommendations*	'Everyday support for a healthier, happier you' (Headspace)
Apple State of Mind	*Symptom and mood tracker*	'Track your mental well-being by logging your moods and emotions, and by taking standardised mental health assessments to understand your current risk of depression and anxiety. If you have concerns about your mental health, consult a clinician' (Apple State of Mind)
Bearable	*Symptom and mood tracker*	'Quick and easy symptom tracking for any chronic health issue or disorder. Discover what improves and worsens your symptoms so that you can find better ways to manage your health and well-being' (Bearable)
aHead	*Therapy bot*	'The Duolingo for your emotional intelligence' (aHead)
Ebb (Headspace)	*Therapy bot*	'Ebb is an empathetic AI companion that helps you navigate life's ups and downs, anytime, anywhere' (Ebb)
Flourish	*Therapy bot*	'Meet Flourish, your science based mental health wellbeing buddy' (Flourish)
Elomia	*Therapy bot*	'Self-care for depression' (Elomia)
MoodMission	*Therapy bot*	'An app for dealing with low moods, stress and anxiety' (Moodmission)
Sensa	*Therapy bot*	'Your mental health is important, Sensa gives you the tools to help you improve it' (Sensa)
Youper	*Therapy bot*	'Youper AI is your Emotional Health Assistant designed to help you feel your best' (Youper)
Wysa	*Therapy bot*	'Mental health redefined' (Wysa)

Therapy bots use established clinical practices to support consumers in managing symptoms of poor mental health. A common support provided through therapy bots is cognitive behavioural therapy ('CBT'). Cognitive behavioural therapy is a form of structured psychotherapy that emphasises identifying and replacing unhelpful thought patterns and behaviours with more adaptive ones. It is used to treat a number of mental health conditions, such as depression, anxiety and eating disorders (InformedHealth.org). The attraction of combining established therapeutic techniques with chatbot functionality is in providing an interactive conversational exchange that engages the user, as opposed to merely directing information at them.

Therapy bots purport to replicate clinical practice, and this means that their interactions with consumers are restricted to conversations that mimic established clinical practice. They do not 'just chat'; they recommend. It appears that consumer users may prefer greater companionship and fewer dictates from their therapy bots. The retention rates of digital mental health tools are relatively low: studies have found that user engagement typically drops off after just fifteen days (Baumel et al., 2019; Adams et al., 2026).

1.2.2 AI Companions

The phenomenon of AI companions refers to app or web-based chatbots that provide 'friendship' through text-based conversation and varying degrees of emotional, romantic and sexual intimacy (Purtill, 2023; Muldoon, 2024). Consumers may create and interact with AI companions in a game-like virtual world experience using avatars they have chosen or designed. Some of the more well-known AI companions and their self-described service are set out in Table 2.

As can be seen from Table 2, AI companions promote their capacity for lifelike interactions. While these interactions may have a purpose of entertainment, they mimic human companionship and may be used in much the same way that humans relate to friends or partners (Bernardi, 2025). Studies have shown that AI companions are being used by consumers for online virtual or imaginary companionship and as a way of exploring social or sexual identity. AI companions are also being used as a resource for responding to relationship problems, loneliness or poor mental health (Cann, 2025). This is a form of support that humans often look to from their friends. It is, therefore, perhaps unsurprising that consumers might also seek this kind of support from an AI companion. Indeed, from the

Table 2 Some popular AI companions

Name of AI Companions	Self-description
Character.ai	'AI chat reimagined' (Character.ai)
Chai.AI	'With our advanced technology, our chatbots think and reply like real characters, complete with authentic voices. ... Whether you're chatting with your favourite celebrity, a beloved character from a movie or TV show, or a historical figure, you'll feel like you're talking to a real person' (Chai.AI)
Kindroid	'Your AI friend with lifelike memory, intelligence, appearances, voices and personalities' (Kindroid)
Pi	'Pi, your personal AI: A Smart and Supportive Companion 24/7' (pi)
Replika	'The AI companion who cares. Always here to listen. Always on your side' (Replika)
Xiaoice	'在亿万人之中，我只属于你' [among billions of people I belong only to you] (Xiaoice)

perspective of consumers, the boundary between AI tools providing mental health support based on established psychological practices and offerings providing companionship may be highly porous.

Both specifically designed therapy bots and AI companions make claims to the kind of insights that might be seen as supporting mental health, at least in the vernacular sense, along with friendship, understanding or care. Notably, some AI companions promote their capacity to address symptoms of poor mental health. For example:

> Feeling down, anxious, having trouble getting to sleep, or managing negative emotions? Replika can help you understand, keep track of your mood, learn coping skills, calm anxiety, work toward positive thinking goals, stress management & much more. Improve your overall mental well-being with your Replika! (Replika, 'What is Replika').

Conversely, therapy bots also promote humanlike interactions that bring them close to the space occupied by AI companions. For example:

> We believe the future combines technology with a human touch to get the most effective and efficient outcomes (Elomia).

> An 'empathetic AI companion [that allows users to u]npack relationship challenges, work stress, sleep issues, and more' (Headspace, 'Meet Ebb').

The mixed messaging in these claims may be confusing for consumers: are they interacting with a lifestyle product with health benefits or a chatbot trained in established psychological techniques? Of course, AI companions only promote companionship. It is possible that consumers may expect a higher level of expertise from general-purpose generative AI chatbots.

1.2.3 Generative AI Chatbots

Outside the relatively specialised services provided by therapy bots and the imaginary friend-like services offered by AI companions, humans are turning to general-purpose generative AI chatbots, such as ChatGPT (OpenAI), Claude (Anthropic) or Gemini (Google), for mental health advice and support (Haensch, 2025; Hall, 2025a; Wallace, 2025a). General-purpose generative AI chatbots are conversational programs powered by generative AI, which is based on large language models. The same models may inform other kinds of chatbots, such as those used specifically for therapy (see 2.2.1). The contrast is that general-purpose chatbots are not restricted to any one particular use.

For consumers, the attractions of using general-purpose generative AI chatbots for mental health may lie in a combination of factors. Generative AI chatbots are easy to access (Cross et al., 2024: 6). They interact in a fluent and conversational style. General-purpose generative AI chatbots do not try to assist users to change their behaviours or suggest therapeutic practices (Wallace, 2025a). It is also possible that consumers hold unrealistic expectations about the level of expertise, responsiveness and care that can be expected from generative AI chatbots given their underlying technology.

2 What Kinds of Technologies Are Being Used?

For many specifically developed therapy bots and other direct-to-consumer digital mental health support tools, 'AI' is a key promoted feature of the offering. For example:

> [We use] a combination of rule-based algorithms and large language modelling to listen and respond intelligently to the thoughts and emotions that you express. As well as listening and responding through conversation, Wysa also recommends skills and techniques that may be helpful for the particular difficulty that you are experiencing. These skills are evidence-based and aim to help you improve your mental resilience and well-being (Wysa FAQ);

> [our] proprietary technology combines psychology and artificial intelligence to understand patients' emotional needs and recommend evidence-based behavioural intervention (Youper).

Although the use of AI is often promoted by developers, the technology that actually underlies the service is rarely described in any detail, and indeed opacity is an issue across the field (Section 3.3.1). This lack of clarity may be for commercial reasons. The underlying technology is also no doubt regularly changing to keep up with more widespread advances in the field. Notably, however, transparency about the underlying architecture is important in identifying the kinds of risks therapy bots and related tools pose and the kinds of laws applying to them.

The following Sections consider the likely technologies used in direct-to-consumer therapy bots and the promoted features of the tools, as well as comparing companion AI and generative AI chatbots.

2.1 'AI' as a Concept

'AI' is a nebulous concept and what is captured by the term in common use has changed as technology advances. At one time, the term was used to describe what are now viewed as simple hand-coded, decision tree-style algorithms. 'AI' has also been used to describe artificial general intelligence, as opposed to narrow AI, which surpasses human intelligence (Manning, 2020). The term 'AI' may describe machine learning algorithms, which use statistical processing techniques to find patterns in large volumes of data from which predictions about future events, proclivities or behaviours can be made (Manning, 2020). More recently, 'AI' has evolved to describe, almost exclusively, generative AI built on large language models, such as text-generating ChatGPT, Gemini or Claude.

The capacities and processes of these various technologies differ, and they may be subject to different guardrails or other protections for users. From the perspective of consumers using therapy bots or other digital mental health tools, the precise technology utilised is less important than the service being provided. Technical boundary-drawing should not distract from the fundamental need for the service to live up to its promoted performance capacity.

2.2 The Underlying Technologies

Therapy bots and other direct-to-consumer digital mental health support tools are commonly promoted on the basis of their capacity to provide personalised recommendations, which means individualised responses to entered information or interactive conversations with consumer users. The different kinds of systems underlying these products are considered in the following sections, noting that they may overlap, and tools may utilise more than one option.

2.2.1 Recommender Systems

Some direct-to-consumer digital mental health support tools rely on recommender systems to provide broadly relevant information to consumers about meditation, mindfulness or other healthy practices (see, e.g., Calm, sign up). The tools collect information about the user through an initial questionnaire and, typically, interactions between the tool and the consumer. This data may then be processed by a machine learning model to provide targeted recommendations based on inferences about the individual user's likely preferences or interests (Chen & Nakamori, 2021). For example, the Headspace mindfulness app is promoted as 'the mental health app for every moment', while the underlying technology is described as follows:

> Machine learning chatbots are core to our user experiences by offering recommendations that engage our users with new relevant, personalized content that builds consistent habits in their lifelong journey (Chen and Nakamori, 2021).

2.2.2 Dashboards

Mood tracking tools rely largely on dashboards to represent information entered by consumers, often combined with recommendations relating to the patterns of behaviour or mood revealed by that information. Even more personalised insights into users' preferences and emotional state might be gleaned from collecting biometric data. In particular, Apple offers an emotion tracking tool that combines insights from biometric data collected from the Apple Watch (Apple). This kind of data is no doubt highly valuable to the developers of the tool, in refining their services, developing new products, for research or commercial endeavour (see further Section 3.2).

2.2.3 Rule-Based, NLP and Generative AI Therapy Chatbots

Recommender systems simply provide content. Chatbots are software programs designed to decode written language and respond appropriately to questions, requests or statements. Chatbot technology allows real-time, responsive interactions with users. Modern chatbots vary in their language capacity (Onlim, 2024; Pierce, 2024).

Chatbots can provide a more interactive experience for consumers, including advice for better mental health and structured therapeutic interventions, such as cognitive behavioural therapy. Chatbots are becoming increasingly prominent forms of digital mental health support, including for example through aHead, Elomia, Youper, Woebot and Wysa. In 2025, the provider of recommendations for mindfulness practices, Headspace, introduced a chatbot, 'Ebb', for well-being and mindfulness support (Headspace, 'Meet Ebb'). AI companions also make use of chatbot technology. For example, 'Replika uses a sophisticated system that combines our own Large Language Model and scripted dialogue content to create more natural and engaging conversations' (Replika, How Does Replika Work).

Chatbots themselves may operate in different ways. Some use rule-based programs to determine their response to statements made by the user, while others combine natural language processing, a form of machine learning, with rule-based systems (Adamopoulou and Moussiades, 2020; Caldarini et al., 2022) and, increasingly, deploy generative AI to inform text-based interactions.

Rule-Based Chatbots

Rule-based chatbots use word or pattern recognition in text that correspond to predefined categories of questions, requests or statements, called 'intents'. The intent will trigger a predetermined response using rules based on if-then-else reasoning (Khanna et al., 2015: 278). Eliza, mentioned at the start of this Element, was a rule-based chatbot. As described by Weizenbaum, 'the program was constructed in a two-tier arrangement, the first tier consisting of the language analyzer and the second of a script' (Weizenbaum, 1976: 3). Decision-tree chatbots are a standard implementation of 'rules-based' chatbots, which prompt the user to select from one of several predefined questions or prompts, with each selection determining the follow-up question or prompt in the fashion of a 'guided conversation' (Pierce, 2024).

NLP Chatbots

Chatbots using natural language processing ('NLP') algorithms (e.g., Siri, Alexa and Google Assistant) use sophisticated statistical techniques to decipher patterns in language instead of relying on predetermined rules written by a human. These chatbots do not understand the language in the sense of deriving meaning from an utterance. Instead, they rely on natural language processing algorithms trained on large volumes of data in order to predict the 'intent' of a human utterance or prompt. At this point, they can provide a response based on predetermined rules or a more free-flowing response to the text based on generative AI. Generative AI has provided chatbots with greater language capacity and adaptivity. They can therefore provide a range of more fluent responses to a human's prompt than rule-based chatbots.

Generative AI Chatbots

Generative AI chatbots are built on large language models and generative pretrained transformer techniques, which together allow for greater language capacity and the ability to generate novel outputs. However, this very generative capacity means that generative AI chatbots are more likely to generate inappropriate or incorrect responses to user queries, sometimes known as 'hallucinations'. The risk of inaccuracy or inappropriate responses can be reduced through a combination of fine-tuning or guardrails placed on the AI. However, many of the generative AI chatbots made available on a free or for-fee basis are trained to prioritise user engagement, which leads to them being described as 'sycophantic'. The combination of a tendency to err combined with a programmed goal of engagement clearly presents risks in mental health contexts and is demonstrated by the increasing numbers of legal actions against the developers of general chatbots and companion AI (Tech Justice Law Project and Social Media Victims Law Center, 2025). By contrast, rule-based approaches and guardrails go some way to ensuring that chatbot therapists respond in ways that are safe and appropriate. However, these restrictions make the chatbots less adaptive and responsive than generally available generative AI chatbots, and for this reason, potentially less attractive to users (Economist, 2025b).

Initially, many of the therapy bots, such as now defunct therapy bot Woebot (Darcy, 2023), as well as Youper and Wysa (Wysa, FAQ), relied on rule-based systems to ensure that the chatbot's responses were kept within designated limits. With this approach comes a certain rigidity of response. Thus, a recent study of Wysa reported that users experienced limitations in the chatbots' understanding of context and a rigid, repetitive conversation style (Chaudhry et al., 2024).

Advances in generative AI in retrieving information and providing naturalistic conversations have seen increasing reliance on this technology. In 2024, Wysa advised that 'we are now integrating Gen AI into Wysa, both to meet user needs and to demonstrate how the risks associated with this technology can be addressed responsibly' (Aggarwal, 2024). Recent entrants to the market, such as Therabot, explicitly refer to the use of generative AI, within appropriate guardrails for a more conversational experience (Economist, 2025b).

2.3 The Promoted Attractions of AI for Mental Health Support

In appealing to consumers, the commonly promoted attractions of therapy bots and other digital mental health tools are their accessibility, capacity for a personalised service and empathy or insight. These promoted features may be more influential in consumers' decision-making about which tool to engage with than the actual technology utilised.

2.3.1 Accessibility and Ease of Use

Direct-to-consumer therapy bots and other direct-to-consumer digital mental health support tools are commonly promoted as offering an easy to use and accessible response to the otherwise unmanageable demand for mental health services. Improving access to psychotherapy was among the attractions attributed to Eliza: 'If the method proves beneficial, then it would provide a therapeutic tool which can be made widely available to member hospitals and psychiatric centres suffering a shortage of therapists' (Weizenbaum, citing Colby, 1976: 5). Similarly, the developers of many current direct-to-consumer mental health support chatbots state a purpose of making mental health care 'accessible for everyone' (Youper). For example:

> We recognised a critical gap in mental health care: while traditional therapy is invaluable, it's not always immediately available when people need support. Our AI bridges this gap, providing immediate support while working alongside traditional mental health services (Elomia Technology).

At their best, direct-to-consumer therapy bots serve people who are not in crisis. This may in turn reduce demands on human mental health professionals, allowing them to respond to more complex or critical cases. These services can be delivered at relatively low cost, at any time and from any location. For some, the attractions of digital mental health support tools go beyond efficiency or accessibility. They may also appeal to consumers with low levels of trust in formal medical systems (Lucas et al., 2014). Young people, in particular, may feel more comfortable receiving mental health support from a chatbot or app (Keirerleber, 2022). Tools that utilise generative AI offer the promise of personalised, expert and convenient support (Ghose, 2021). They appear to allow anonymity (consider whether the extensive data collection practices accompanying these tools genuinely allow this), seem empathetic, and are never judgmental.

These promoted attractions of direct-to-consumer therapy are in some ways amplified for AI companions and general-purpose generative AI. Not only are the latter options easily available; companion AI and general-purpose generative AI chatbots carry no agenda of encouraging the consumer to 'work' towards better mental health, they appear purely to entertain or serve. And they are sometimes said to 'know' the needs of the consumer user.

2.3.2 Personalisation

Therapy bots and other direct-to-consumer digital mental health support tools are often promoted for their capacity to provide a personalised response to consumers as opposed to the generic (and often static) information provided through online portals or webpages (Chen & Nakamori, 2021; Robb, 2024). Therapy bots, in particular, are promoted not merely as offering 'off the shelf' content but also as using technology to tailor material directly to 'you', the consumer.

For example:

> [Ebb is] an empathetic AI companion that helps you navigate life's ups and downs, anytime, anywhere (Headspace, Meet Ebb).

> Youper's proprietary technology combines psychology and artificial intelligence to understand patients' emotional needs and recommend evidence-based behavioural interventions (Youper).

This promoted capacity for personalisation in therapy bots may be more limited than the headline statements of the developers suggest, and may not correspond with consumers' expectations.

Notably, the data profiles on which direct-to-consumer therapy bots and other direct-to-consumer digital mental health support tools rely are not drawn from the personal knowledge that might arise from the interactions that occur between health professionals and consumers. Instead, responses are based on statistical correlations between the individual user and the profiles or segments drawn from the training data to develop the digital mental health support tool. Thus, recommendations or predictions based on data profiles are only ever an approximation of what might be suitable for individual consumers because the data is merely a proxy for the attribute the tools are trying to predict (Hildebrandt, 2022). Generative AI works in a similar way, because any response to a human prompt is based on probabilities learnt from the training data set not a deep understanding of language, or emotion. Nonetheless, the combination of an interactive conversation and personalised content may give rise to an impression that therapy bots 'care' about their consumer users.

2.3.3 Empathy, Expertise and Insight

Along with personalisation, the promotion for direct-to-consumer digital mental health tools often stresses the capacity of their chatbot offerings for empathy, expertise and insight. For example:

> Think of us as your emotional companion, someone who's there for you every day, not just in moments of crisis. We're like that friend who

> truly listens, helps you untangle your thoughts, celebrates your wins, and gives you a gentle nudge when you need it. Our role is to support you in building emotional skills, forming healthier habits, and feeling more grounded in your daily life (aHead, FAQ).
>
> Ebb is an empathetic AI companion that helps you navigate life's ups and downs, anytime, anywhere (Headspace, Meet Ebb).

The marketing for AI companions similarly often emphasises their capacity for humanlike emotion. For example:

> [designed to show] empathy and understanding (Kindroid);
>
> supportive, empathetic, and intelligent conversational AI (Pi).

Consumers may attribute similar characteristics even to general generative AI chatbots. Research by Myra Cheng et al. has found that US consumers 'perceive AI as warm and competent' (Cheng, 2026b).

Opinions may differ on whether humans should be turning to chatbots for mental health advice. Specialist therapy bots may provide useful mental health advice, as indeed may companion AI and general-purpose generative AI chatbots (Gilbert, 2025). It is less clear they provide empathy or care. For a consumer, talking to a chatbot might *feel* like talking to a friend or therapist. But AI chatbots are neither friends nor therapists in the way those terms are normally understood. AI chatbots only ever mimic human manifestations of care, empathy or other interpersonal interactions; they do not feel them (Paterson, 2025). For consumers, mimicked emotion may not detract from the sense of connection they experience in interacting with a chatbot. Humans interacting with Eliza found the experience meaningful. Nonetheless, there may be normative objections to this kind of 'fabricated' interaction (Ciriello et al., 2024; Sharkey & Sharkey, 2021).

AI chatbots cannot exhibit the sort of genuine empathy that comes with friendship or the insight that comes with a genuine therapeutic relationship between a human health professional. It seems problematic and even misleading to suggest the contrary. Additionally, AI companions and generative AI chatbots are commercial products sometimes made available for a fee or at the cost of personal data collection for training, which must affect any loyalty they might show to the human consumer.

Relatedly, although they may purport to 'care', AI companions and general generative AI chatbots have no purported expertise in the field of mental health. Indeed, companion AI and generative AI chatbots have been criticised for failing to recognise and appropriately respond to suicidal ideation (Turc, 2022; Daws, 2020; Atillah, 2023; Xiang, 2023a; Duffy, 2024) or even encouraging such behaviours (Duffy, 2025; Chatterjee, 2025). Generative AI chatbots have a tendency to sycophancy, in the sense of reflecting back the apparent preferences of the user, which Myra Cheng et al. observe is harmful to 'social judgment' (Cheng et al., 2026a) and has led to reports of AI psychosis (Hudon & Stip, 2025; Moore et al., 2026).

At this point in time when AI is relatively new, there is therefore considerable scope for humans to misunderstand the nature of their relationship with a chatbot therapist, who has neither insight nor empathy for the human, even if they are able to offer suggestions for better mental health that have some validity (Khawaja & Bélisle-Pipon, 2023). Weizenbaum himself worried that 'if, as appears to be the case, the public's attributions are wildly misconceived, then public decisions are bound to be misguided and often wrong' (1976: 8). Perhaps the somewhat confused nature of the relationship between humans and AI therapy bots might be forgiven if these tools are providing significant therapeutic benefits. However, therapy bots carry a number of as yet unresolved risks and limitations.

3 Risks and Regulation for Therapy Bots

Specifically designed therapy bots might prove effective in providing assistance to consumers who are experiencing poor mental health or want to sustain a general sense of well-being. However, as yet, these effects remain to be securely established, even more so with AI companions or general-purpose generative AI. There are other risks of use as well, going beyond utility and covering failures in data protection, bias, error and one-sided contract terms that shift risk to consumers. All of these possible harms are concerning, but in many cases, there are laws and regulation that should mitigate the risks. As the following discussion shows, however, these regimes are infrequently and unevenly applied.

Part of the issue is that therapy bots, and other direct-to-consumer digital mental health support tools, operate across several key legal categories: therapeutic goods, confidentiality/data privacy, AI and online safety and consumer protection. These categories can be used as a lens for understanding the risks that the products may present for consumers and organising the various legal responses. It is useful to consider each category separately, and previous scholarly work has focused particularly on risks to privacy and of therapeutic benefit in the use of digital mental health support tools. However, this should not be taken to mean there is an impenetrable dividing line between the categories. Assessing the risks and benefits of the tools requires an understanding of their operation across legal categories. Additionally, as argued in Section 4, an effective regulatory response to the risks and opportunities of therapy bots must move beyond legal silos.

The next Section assesses the operation of therapy bots and related direct-to-consumer digital mental health support tools, as well as companion AI and general-purpose generative AI chatbots, through the lens of therapeutic benefit, confidentiality/data privacy, responsible AI and consumer protection. It also considers the application of relevant law in these categories.

3.1 Therapeutic Benefit

A first lens for considering the benefits and risks of direct-to-consumer digital mental health tools is therapeutic benefit. In making assertions about assisting with mental health in their marketing and promotional materials, the developers of therapy bots and other direct-to-consumer digital mental health support tools implicitly, if not expressly, represent that the tools are effective in reducing the symptoms of poor mental health or improving overall well-being. Certainly, cognitive behavioural therapy, commonly the underlying basis for direct-to-consumer therapy bots, has a strong evidence base in its core applications when delivered by trained professionals (Hofmann et al., 2012).

However, cognitive behavioural therapy does not always work well for consumers or for some conditions. It requires a close therapeutic relationship between consumers and therapists, as well as a commitment to the practice by consumers. The effectiveness of mindfulness practices as a response to symptoms of poor mental health is less well established, even when delivered in person, still less online (see, for example, the MYRIAD study of school-aged children (Kuyken et al., 2022)).

It is possible that therapy bots and other direct-to-consumer digital mental health support tools will show a similar pattern of outcomes. It is also possible that the products work best when used in conjunction with human mental health professionals. The clinical results may also be different for digital tools used without human interaction or oversight. Human therapists may simply provide services with more insight and compassion than an artificial agent (Tasioulas, 2022: 237). In the context of mental health, Tekin notes that '[b]uilding a therapeutic alliance is a relational process, in which the therapist gives uptake to the patient's concerns, and the patient feels recognized and cared for' (Tekin, 2021: 456). Tekin is sceptical that 'this type of alliance can be formed between a person and a bot' (Tekin, 2021: 456). Achtyes et al. express concern that direct-to-consumer mental health chatbots may even have harmful consequences such as misdiagnoses and delayed treatment (Achtyes et al., 2023: 265–266).

These observations do not rule out the possibility that well-designed direct-to-consumer interventions may play a role in improving access to mental health support in a way that is both safe and meaningful for consumers and professionals. However, they underline the importance of testing, review and oversight of the products.

3.1.1 Studies and Surveys

There is relatively little empirical or clinical evidence about the long-term performance of therapy bots and other direct-to-consumer digital mental health support tools. This may not be surprising given the products are relatively new to the market. But it does mean they should not be over-promoted by developers.

Clinical Studies of Direct-to-Consumer Digital Mental Health Tools

Several developers of digital mental health support tools seek to promote the effectiveness of their products by reference to 'scientific' backing in the form of clinical research studies. For example:

> MoodMission's [mindfulness exercises] are taken from scientific research, made accessible to you through the app, so you can learn exactly how what you're doing is helping (MoodMission).

> [Headspace mindfulness and mental health chatbot is] the leading mental health companion, but the only way to know if we're truly accomplishing that is to measure, test, and study its impact. That's where our research comes in (Headspace, Science at Headspace).

These kinds of scientific support claims are commonly overstated, with headline statements exaggerating the probity of the findings. For example, mindfulness support tool provider, Headspace, refers to the benefits of meditation in responding to anxiety and regulating emotions as follows:

> Anxiety is a cognitive state connected to an inability to regulate emotions … a consistent meditation practice reprograms neural pathways in the brain and, therefore, improves our ability to regulate emotions (Headspace meditation).

Notably, the study cited by Headspace in support of this statement did not involve meditation apps. It covered experienced meditation practitioners who, on average, 'had 9.1 ± 7.1 years of meditation experience and practiced 6.2 ± 4.0 h per week' as well as having participated in an 'at least 1 week-long Insight meditation retreat, which entails approximately 10 h of meditation per day' (Lazar et al., 2005: 1894).

> Published studies, external scientists, prestigious research organizations and our science team have shown Headspace can improve mental, emotional, and social health (Headspace, Science Blog).

Some of the Headspace studies do report positive outcomes for app use, for example, in reducing mind-wandering (Bennike et al., 2017), producing compassion (Lim et al., 2015) or reducing depression (Flett et al., 2019) and stress (Bostock et al., 2018). However, there are limitations to these studies. Some were conducted by Headspace researchers, reducing their independence (Economides et al., 2018. See also Cachia et al., 2025, discussing Flourish). Other Headspace studies involved small, discrete cohorts of users or produced only qualified findings (Wylde et al., 2017) or negligibly positive outcomes (Noone & Hogan, 2018). The published Headspace studies typically only tracked app use over a short period of time.

The marketing for other direct-to-consumer digital mental health support tools that purport to rely on 'scientific' studies show similar limitations (Economist, 2025b). Systematic reviews of published studies on the digital mental health support tools have found only limited effectiveness (Marshall et al., 2020). Chandrashekar reports that, for products treating depression and anxiety for which clinical trials that have been conducted, meta-analysis of outcomes reveals that there are benefits for particular cohorts and not others: 'smartphone-based therapies yield the greatest benefits for individuals with mild to moderate, rather than major, depression'. As for 'anxiety-focused mobile tools', these 'delivered the greatest reductions in anxiety symptoms when paired with face-to-face or internet-based therapies' (Chandrashekar, 2018: 2; see also Cross et al., 2023: 302–305). Goldberg et al. suggest that, at most, existing studies showed a 'proof of concept':

> Taken together, these results suggest that mobile phone-based interventions may hold promise for modestly reducing common psychological symptoms (e.g., depression, anxiety), although effect sizes are generally small and rarely do these interventions outperform other interventions intended to be therapeutic (i.e., specific active controls) (Goldberg et al., 2020: 15).

A further concern that has been raised about many of the studies of direct-to-consumer digital mental health support tools is their omission of any 'discussion of adverse events' that might cast doubt on 'the safety of these interventions' (Goldberg et al., 2020: 15). Torous et al. suggest that adverse outcomes for consumers using the tools are not well reported (Torous, 2025: 159. Also Department of Health, 2021: 10). Direct-to-consumer digital mental health support tools have not been well investigated for use by people from often marginalised groups, such as from linguistically or culturally diverse communities and neurodivergent people, nor developed with users (Balcombe, 2026). Furthermore, such products do not themselves address the social conditions that may create and escalate mental distress in their users (Mathias, 2022; Tekin, 2021: 457).

User engagement with digital mental health support tools has been shown to be difficult to sustain and tends to decline in a matter of weeks (Torous et al., 2025). Lowrey (2021) notes that in the reported studies, app 'attrition rates are high'. Research by Valentine et al. (2025) found that there was no standardised measure for tracking engagement. The drop in engagement is most apparent with static tools, mood tracking and recommender apps (Baumel et al., 2019), perhaps due to a level of user frustration over their lack of responsiveness (Haque & Rubya, 2022). Thus, for example, one study found that 'nearly half of the participants allocated to the popular Headspace and Smiling Mind apps reported never using the app again after ten days' (Torous et al., 2025: 163, citing Flett et al., 2019).

It may be that therapy bots are more engaging and effective. A randomised controlled trial of generative AI therapy bot, Therabot, found sustained engagement over four weeks and positive outcomes for participants over eight weeks in reducing the symptoms of a major depressive disorder (Heinz, 2025), while recognising the need for further research (see also Gratch & Essig, 2025). However, to the extent that the focus of even generative AI therapy bots is therapeutic interventions, such as CBT, they still may prove less compelling to users than the more conversational, and even sycophantic, interactions with an AI companion or general-purpose generative AI chatbots (Wallace, 2025a).

Overall, Torous et al. conclude that:

> Despite significant advancements …, recent industry failures and research critiques have highlighted the need for more rigorous approaches, including use of AI placebos in controlled trials, generalizable and

> pre-registered chatbots, and greater transparency in data sharing. Much of recent research has focused on how a particular app or artificial intelligence program might work but has not produced mechanistic and generalizable evidence that the field can utilize to build a strong scientific base. (2025: 156)

In many therapeutic contexts, these kinds of studies would be demanded to establish the efficacy and safety of a product. They would be relevant to being assessed and approved by the therapeutic goods regulators responsible for drugs and diagnostic devices. However, as discussed in 3.1.2, therapy bots and other direct-to-consumer mental health support tools have largely been treated as outside therapeutic regimes, largely because they continue to be viewed as low-risk 'lifestyle' products. Even if more is demanded, random clinical trials take time and may fail to overcome the lack of user overall engagement with direct-to-consumer digital mental health support tools. In the interim, specialised products may be overtaken by interactions with AI companions or general-purpose generative AI chatbots, for which there is no expectation or promise of clinical efficacy.

Studies on the Impact of AI Companions

AI companions may be viewed as a fantasy world encounter, but they are promoted as having real-world impacts such as companionship or reducing loneliness (Reddit, Replika Official and Reddit, Stanford Study). The empirical literature on the mental health effects of AI companions is nascent but developing in response to well-publicised examples of AI companions encouraging self-harm. A study by Zhang et al. suggested companion AI use is associated with lower levels of well-being, especially for already isolated individuals, concluding they are not a substitute for human connection (Zhang et al., 2025). De Freitas et al. found that AI companions can help alleviate loneliness but observed that, in the longer term, the apps may create dependencies that work against well-being (De Freitas et al., 2026; also, Maples et al., 2024). The longer-term outcomes of these interactions are less clear (Economist, 2025b). Several studies have found that AI companion apps and generative AI chatbots are poor at identifying and responding to signs of distress or suicidal ideation in users (De Freitas et al., 2024; Pichowicz, 2025). While there is little empirical or clinical research on the impact of generative AI chatbots used for mental health, at the time of writing reports of AI induced psychosis have begun to emerge (Hudon & Stip, 2025; Moore, et al., 2026).

3.1.2 Regulating Therapeutic Products

Therapeutic devices, such as products used to diagnose and treat medical conditions, are typically subject to safety protocols imposed by drug or therapeutic goods laws. These laws are in turn overseen by designated regulators such as the Therapeutic Goods Administration ('TGA') in Australia, the Medicines and Healthcare Products Regulatory Agency ('MHRA') in the UK or the Food and Drug Administration ('FDA') in the US.[1] The goal of regulators is to ensure that medical devices are effective and safe before entering the market. Product safety requirements for medical devices are scaled according to the assessed risk of the product, with higher risk products requiring clinical evaluation (e.g. randomised controlled trials), documentation and monitoring.[2]

The therapeutic device regulators in the US, UK and Australia have tended to exercise only a light-touch regulatory approach to digital mental health support tools. In this regard, the approach taken by the FDA in the US has been influential, given that many therapy bots have been developed in that jurisdiction (Duggal et al., 2018; Wallace & Pestaina, 2023). In 2016, following changes to its constituent legislation, the FDA stated it would not regulate devices intended only 'for maintaining or encouraging a healthy lifestyle' (Food and Drug Administration, 2016, 2026).

So-called 'wellness' tools have typically been subject to minimal regulatory oversight on the ground that they do not fall within the FDA category of medical device (Shuren et al., 2018). This approach has been justified by the FDA on the grounds that 'active FDA oversight would provide little to no public health value while unnecessarily delaying patient access to potentially beneficial technologies' (Shuren et al., 2018: 338). This approach has been criticised. Scatterday argues that it represents a policy decision to 'decrease the "regulatory burdens" associated with app development to drive marketplace innovation and

---

[1] For discussion of the EU medical device scheme and its application to AI mental health tools, see Steindl (2023: 212–213).

[2] Outside the therapeutic goods regime, goods may be subject to general product safety regimes (e.g., Australian Consumer Law 2010 part 3-3; General Product Safety Regulations 2005 (UK); Consumer Product Safety Act (US)). Depending on the jurisdiction, these regimes impose requirements for certain products to meet specified safety standards and reporting of product-related injuries. Product safety regimes do not usually extend to 'pure' services (i.e., those that are provided online as opposed to being part of a good such as a GPS). This leaves out digital health support tools that are provided as services.

technological advancement' (2022: 653; see also, Taylor, 2021: 2281). Mattioli observes that since the FDA 'put its waiver into effect, makers of unapproved apps branded as "wellness" tools rebranded their products as medical interventions' (Mattioli, 2021: 10). Torous et al. observe that 'well over 99% of publicly available mental health related apps [are] marketing themselves as well-being and not health devices' (Torous, 2025: 160).

A similar approach has been taken in Australia and the UK. In both jurisdictions, tools that are considered 'health products' (Department of Health, Disability and Aging, 2025), and do not involve 'assessing risk, diagnosing, predicting, monitoring, treating or preventing mental health conditions and/or symptoms', are outside the 'software as a medical device designation' (MHRA, 2025: 10). Examples of such tools include sports performance (MHRA, 2025: 8, 17) and healthy sleep monitoring (MHRA, 2025: 16). In Australia, there is an exception for tools that are 'based on established clinical guidelines that are referenced and displayed in the software in a manner that is reviewable by the user' (Department of Health, Disability and Ageing, 2024).

More recently, the FDA has addressed the interest in using generative AI to inform mental health support tools, and the rise of AI therapists. In 2025, the FDA committed to ongoing oversight recognising that:

> The utilization of generative AI within digital mental health medical devices may offer unique benefits to patients and public health, but their use and adoption also comes with specific risks and complexities that necessitate careful consideration of effective and tailored approaches to regulatory oversight. (Food and Drug Administration, 2025: 17).

The UK regulator has released guidance that includes considering the level of functionality of a mental health tool in classification for the purposes of the regulatory regime (MHRA, 2025: 13). This means a tool using a chatbot for interactions will have higher functionality, and hence more stringent oversight, than a tool that provides information as fixed text (MHRA, 2025: 22–23). In Australia, the TGA recommended a review into digital mental health tools using AI, considering that the current exclusions from regulation may no longer be appropriate (Department of Health, Disability and Ageing, 2025). In the UK, regulatory guidance considers promotional material in characterising the device as falling inside or outside the 'software as a medical device regime' (MHRA, 2025: 8, 17), and this has also been suggested in Australia (Department of Health, Disability and Ageing, 2025: 13). It is clear that more research and clinical evidence on the efficacy and safety of digital mental health tools in responding to anxiety and depression is required (Torous et al., 2025). Such research takes time and, in the interim, there is still a need for the products to be acceptably safe.

In this light, statements that the products produce genuine therapeutic or clinical benefits should be viewed with caution. Therapy bots and other direct-to-consumer digital mental health tools are not mediated through trained health professionals who could explain the limitations of the underlying studies or assess whether the product is suitable for a given user. This context may justify demands for care in promotional statements, or even support concerns that some promotional statements pointing to qualified health benefits are misleading. This is a topic that is considered in more detail in Section 3.4.2. The absence of a medical practitioner in providing mental health support also raises issues of privacy and confidentiality, along with data protection.

3.2 Data Privacy and Confidentiality

A second lens for considering the risks, and legal/regulatory responses, associated with therapy bots and other direct-to-consumer digital mental health support tools is data privacy and confidentiality. Mental health support tools not only typically sit outside therapeutic goods regimes; because they are provided directly to consumers, they also fall outside the stringent legal and ethical duties of confidentiality that attach to therapists. This in itself may surprise consumers, although it may still be possible to argue that information provided to a therapy bot should be treated as confidential as this was the obvious intention behind the disclosure.

The harms that may arise from voluminous data collection, insecure storage and broad data sharing practices, such as reputational, psychological, autonomy and discrimination harms (Citron & Solove, 2022), clearly have a resonance in the context of mental health support tools. Here the sharing, leaking or theft of sensitive personal mental health data will clearly be unsettling to individuals, or may place them at personal or professional risk (see Clifford et al., 2022). Data sharing practices raise legitimate concerns about the risk of discrimination, such as in insurance, employment or access to government benefits (World Economic Forum and Deloitte, 2021: 17–18; Steindl, 2023). Concerns about such risks may reduce trust in such tools for the future, even where they may potentially be helpful (see Dove et al., 2026). Data protection law provides some response; although, as discussed in Section 4, it works best in co-ordination with other regimes.

This Section considers practices that intrude on privacy or confidentiality and the regulatory responses available.

3.2.1 Data Practices

Any product claiming to provide personalised recommendations will rely on collected and processed personal data to some degree, and in the case of therapy bots and other digital mental health support tools, potentially sensitive personal data about health-related matters. Indeed, this lies at the heart of these kinds of self-monitoring or self-help tools. Ghose (2021) describes health support tools generally as leading to 'the "quantified self", a phenomenon where individuals start tracking their behavioural, physiological, biological, and other kinds of health markers'. Flore (2023: 39) describes mental health and well-being tools as enacting 'self-care in a moment of habitual data tracking and monitoring'. Consumers engaging with such tools will understand they are sharing sensitive personal data and have an expectation that data will be kept securely and stored discreetly. They may not understand the breadth of data being collected nor the uses made of that data.

Data Collected

Most digital mental health support tools collect personal information such as the user's name, email address, age and gender directly from the user. Some mental health, well-being and mindfulness tools also collect data from third-party tools, social media and online conduct. For example, Calm (a mindfulness app) collects data from advertising partners, research platforms, business contact databases, geolocation data, internet activity and browsing behaviour; and draws inferences from this data on a user's product interests to obtain purchasing insights (Calm Privacy Policy). Youper (a mental health chatbot) collects user files such as photos and videos, lists of friends, likes and other social media activity to create a detailed profile of their users (Youper, Privacy Policy).

The breadth of the data collected may come as a surprise to many consumers, who may reasonably expect their profiles to be limited to information that they have directly provided and not the inferred information from their device use or social media interactions. These sources of data may raise concerns about the accuracy of the individual consumer profile created and undermine consumers' control over the data they provide about themselves.

Data Shared

The developers of therapy bots and related digital mental health support tools may not actually *sell* data, and most probably do not;[3] but data *sharing* practices are widespread in the field. A number of tools use personal data for targeted marketing, including disclosing that information to marketing companies. For example, Calm, Youper and Headspace's privacy policies reveal that personal data is used for marketing, which allows for user targeting. Targeted advertising is problematic in the context of mental health support. This is because the very sending of advertisements promoting mental health support may conceivably trigger symptoms in those experiencing poor mental health. Such advertising may also employ insights revealed by users to manipulate their preferences with the aim of encouraging them to buy more products provided by the company or its affiliates. Users may opt out of targeted advertising by changing their preferences on Google or on social media, but this is not a preferred 'privacy by design' approach, which would instead require an opt-in approach to targeted advertising.

Some digital mental health support tools offer the option for a sponsor, such as an employer, school or university, to provide the app to its employees or students for free or at a reduced rate.[4] The quid pro quo of this arrangement is that those tools may share data with the third-party sponsors. For example:

> In limited cases, we may provide certain personal information to your Benefit Sponsor, including your name, email address, your registration date, and the date on which you last used our Platform. Generally, we restrict this sharing to not include specific details of your in-app activity or any details about your use of Services, like therapy. This restriction may not apply where sharing some of your activity is necessary for your treatment, payment, or healthcare operations such as if your Benefit Sponsor is your other healthcare provider, health insurance provider, or health plan) (Headspace, Privacy Policy).

> Sometimes, your Institutions or their appointed representatives might share or ask you to share your personal data with the app, like your contact details, so we can offer you our services. Where required by your Institution, and without affecting your rights, We [sic] may also share your usage and safety data with them (Wysa, Privacy Policy).

---

[3] Although as Kemp (2023: 13) notes, personal data collected by health support tools may be sold as a business asset, either on its own or as part of a sale of the whole business.

[4] Email sent to students at a sponsoring university stating, 'For the rest of 2022, you can access the Headspace app for free!' (on file with author).

This degree of sharing may be beyond consumers' expectations, and if understood, may reduce consumers' willingness to use the tool under workplace plans.

Many of the privacy policies of therapy bots and related tools state that consumers' data will be shared for research purposes, which are then used to promote the quality of the product (Headspace, Privacy Policy). Research based on app data may have many benefits to consumers, such as improving understandings about the role of such tools in mental health and improving their efficacy. There is also interest in using data from smartphone interactions for digital phenotyping, which uses the contextual data collected from ubiquitous computing methods (such as smartphone interactions) to 'objectively monitor mental health' (Moura et al., 2023). Consumers may feel comfortable with some of these uses and not others. The term 'research' reveals little about the scope of the intended use of the data. Moreover, it gives little indication of how and by whom the research may be done. Universities typically mandate that organisations must follow certain guidelines when using individuals' personal data for medical research (National Health and Medical Research Council, 2024). Yet Kemp (2023) argues that, in the context of 'femtech' tools for ovulation and fertility tracking, sharing for 'research' purposes is an ambiguous phrase that does not guarantee that the data will be used for research approved through the ethics procedures used by publicly funded research institutions and universities.

In most cases, only de-identified or anonymised information and aggregated data are shared with researchers and sponsors; but even this use may cause discomfort to some users. It is not clear from the privacy policies what methods are used to anonymise or de-identify data. De-identification typically only involves the removal of that information which meets the criteria of 'personal information'. Other identifiers, such as IP address or information 'relating to an individual' that would enable easy identification, are not removed from the shared dataset (Kemp, 2023: 18). Additionally, re-identification of anonymised data is recognised as an increasingly straightforward process, particularly with smaller data sets or for individuals who are outliers in the data (Culnane et al., 2019; Hern, 2019). Aggregation of data is also not free from risk for consumers. Aggregation allows third parties to drive insights into predicted behaviours and preferences (Parker et al., 2019a: 198–199), which can then be used to price consumer products and determine access to goods and services (Pasquale, 2015: 206).

3.2.2 Data Privacy Laws

Consumers of therapy bots and related mental health support tools may have some protections against harms arising from data breaches, unauthorised sharing or other misuse of personal information under data protection legislation. As in other areas, one functional limitation of these measures lies in consent, which may legitimate data collection despite being obtained through arguably manipulative practices.

Private Rights of Action

There are a number of options for private rights of action by consumers of therapy bots in circumstances where their personal data has been misused. Consumers may be able to pursue private rights of action under data protection regimes, privacy torts or actions for breach of confidence, which some argue can be drawn on to formulate a nascent approach to fiduciary-like duties held by data controllers (Dove et al., 2026). Where the privacy policy does not match actual practice, consumers may have claims for misrepresentation, as well as being supported by possible regulator action. This strategy has already been successful against digital platforms (see, e.g., Fair, 2019; Paterson et al., 2024) and games provider Fortnite (FTC, 2022). In 2023 the FTC issued a proposed order banning BetterHelp, which provides an online counselling service, from sharing consumers' health data for advertising contrary to the terms of its own privacy policy (FTC, 2023b). This followed enforcement action in 2021 against Flo Health, an app for tracking menstrual and fertility cycles, for sharing data with third parties contrary to its privacy policy (FTC, 2021b). However, the issue in this context arises less from unauthorised data sharing than from overreaching privacy policies that may allow such conduct.

Consent and Deceptive Design Techniques

Many developers of therapy bots and related digital mental health support tools disclose in their privacy policies that they collect data from a variety of sources and list the ways in which that data may be shared or used (albeit in sometimes vague terms). The privacy policies seek consent to these practices from consumers at the time of signing up. Seeking consent reduces the threat of enforcement action by regulators for unauthorised sharing of personal data. However, it is unlikely to inform the decisions of consumers (Federal Trade Commission, 2021a). As this information is only disclosed in the fine print of a privacy policy, consumers may not be aware of their support tool's data practices. This means that when answering questions about their mental health, sleep cycle and productivity patterns, consumers may not realise this sensitive information will be collected, used and shared, including potentially with employers or for training generative AI chatbots. There should be greater clarity from mental health and well-being tools about their sharing practices and the opportunity for users to opt out of these practices, or better still, to opt in. For example, it may be useful to implement a pop-up notification that informs consumers, at the point of interacting with certain features, about the nature of the data they may be sharing with the app and seeks their consent to process such information.

There is also a prevalence of 'deceptive design' techniques (Consumer Policy Research Centre, 2022; Norwegian Consumer Council, 2018) in the user interfaces of therapy bots, and other direct-to-consumer digital mental health support tools, which may amplify concerns about overreaching data collection and barriers to consumers who seek to leave these platforms (Ananthapadmanaban & Paterson, 2023). For example, the sign-up processes for some tools are overreaching in exploiting the 'free trial' period, bundling or inferring consent or using dark patterns to nudge users attempting to unsubscribe against following through on this decision. These problematic practices are in most cases deliberate design choices and are neither necessary nor inevitable in providing digital mental health support in a commercial setting. Increasingly, many countries are taking deliberate action to prohibit deceptive design choices (Ananthapadmanaban & Paterson, 2026). The overarching imperative, however, is that concerns about the privacy impacts of data sharing practices are not resolved merely by demanding clearer privacy policies or putting faith in increasingly stringent concepts of consent, but rather by facilitating the fuller conception of responsibility and agency, as promoted in Bosua et al. (2025: 44).

Consumers might, in some circumstances, be prepared to trade personal data for digital mental health support. But this trade-off assumes that the underlying technologies are safe, accurate and free from objectionable bias to an acceptable level, having regard to their function. There is a circularity to the problems of data protection in this space. More training and stronger guardrails may improve the capacity of therapy bots, as well as the general-purpose AI chatbots or companions being used to support consumer mental health and well-being. Yet the apparently simple suggestion of collecting more training data to ensure AI chatbots are responsive to mental health challenges raises another concern. Consumers using mental health tools, companion AI apps or generative AI chatbots are already sharing large amounts of personal and sensitive data to obtain the support they seek, potentially eroding privacy in a field that carries considerable stigma and possible vulnerability to manipulation by unscrupulous commercial developers of such tools. These issues would, ideally, be addressed by frameworks for ethical, safe and responsible AI.

3.3 Ethical, Safe and Responsible AI

A third lens for assessing the risks of and responses to therapy bots and related direct-to-consumer digital mental health support tools lies in the extent to which such products are designed and deployed in a way that meets emerging standards for ethical, safe and responsible AI (Coghlan et al., 2023; Parviainen & Rantala, 2022). The ideal of ethical AI is informed by an aspiration to thoughtful design and deployment that enriches the lives of the humans dealing with it (Halsband & Heinrichs, 2022; OECD, 2024). There are many formulations of ethics principles, and they may be expressed in different ways (European Commission, 2019). Nonetheless, there are some common themes (Mittelstadt et al., 2016; Jobin et al., 2019; Tsamados et al., 2022), including transparency, explainability and accountability, as well as fairness and inclusion (National Artificial Intelligence Centre, 2024). These latter requirements mean ensuring AI-informed products do not discriminate against groups based on protected attributes and that diverse stakeholder perspectives are accommodated, with regard paid to the experiences and expertise of groups that are often marginalised or experience vulnerability (National Artificial Intelligence Centre, 2024: 43). AI safety is sometimes associated with the existential risk of AI threatening the future of humanity. As a concept, it also applies to a commitment to protecting those who may be subject to AI-informed decisions or practices which materially impact their lives. Principles of responsible AI overlap with those for ethical and safe AI, and further emphasise good governance and accountability for AI that is deployed in contexts affecting humans.

Principles for ethical, safe and responsible AI have been criticised as an ineffective measure for ensuring that AI-informed products genuinely benefit and do not harm humans. They may be too easily dismissed. Although not legally binding, such principles can inform decision-making about AI design, development and deployment. They may further have a 'horizontal' effect in influencing how existing laws are applied to AI developers and deployers. Commitments to ethical, safe and responsible AI are also embodied in governance instruments, technical standards (see, e.g., IEEE, CertifAIEd), risk management frameworks that increasingly inform expectations of good corporate governance (see, e.g., Australian Voluntary AI Safety Standard, 2024) and legislation (see, e.g., EU *AI Act*, 2024).

The following Section considers the AI-specific harms that principles of ethical AI seek to redress and the legal responses to those kinds of concerns.

3.3.1 AI-Specific Harms

In the main, principles of ethical and safe AI seem to have had little impact on the design or deployment of digital mental health tools. Through the lens of ethical, safe and responsible AI principles, the key risks associated with therapy bots and other digital mental health support tools are bias and errors, inaccuracies and inappropriate content and opacity or lack of transparency. Failure to engage with these principles may result in products that are, at best, ineffective for some groups of users and, at worst, unsafe.

Bias and Failures of Inclusion

Bias is a significant concern in the outputs of AI, whether that be generative AI or predictive analytics based on machine learning algorithms. The concept of algorithmic bias expresses the risks of amplifying and replicating existing discrimination arising from human-based decision-making and social policies or practices. Data that reflects historical discrimination will replicate that in data-driven outcomes (Barocas & Selbst, 2016). Unjustified bias in outcomes may also arise where data is not representative of social demographics or when a model trained on data from one context is applied outside those key parameters (Tsamados et al., 2022: 220; Leslie et al., 2021).

Concerns about unfair bias have been identified in the use of AI in numerous health contexts (see, e.g., Bichell & Anthony, 2021; Davis, 2021; Koplin et al., 2025; Valbuena et al., 2022), including mental health (Cross et al., 2024: 2). In the context of therapy bots, a primary concern relates to advice that perpetuates discriminatory stereotypes to the disadvantage of already marginalised people, such as people from low socioeconomic status, culturally and linguistically diverse backgrounds or people with disabilities. Automated technologies may give unsuitable advice to people in these groups because they have not been considered in the tool's design or included in the training data.

Strong precautionary responses to algorithmic bias require processes and policies implemented in the technology's design, development and deployment to reduce the potential for harm. These might, for example, include care in testing, reviewing and cleaning the data; auditing outcomes to look for patterns of disadvantage for protected attributes or groups; counterfactuals or weightings to identify factors that distort outcomes; and ongoing governance to ensure complaints are responded to and reviewed. It is not unreasonable to expect these issues to be addressed in the governance of digital mental health support tools (see, e.g., Department of Health, 2021: 9). Going further, we might also expect a commitment to inclusion and equity to ensure that the tools are suitable *by design* for the breadth of the cohort who might use them (Zowghi et al., 2024).

Some developers of therapy bots do explicitly recognise concerns of diversity or bias. For example:

> Ebb has been rigorously tested through exercises specifically designed to identify and mitigate potential biases (Headspace, Meet Ebb).

> We design our products and services with accessibility and inclusivity in mind (Wysa, Accessibility Policy).

> Wysa 'tests rollouts' to ensure Gen AI is free of 'unfair or biased statements' (Aggarwal, 2024).

None of the tools appear to evince a commitment to involving people with lived experience of mental illness or poor mental health in their design (Gilbert, 2025).

Errors, Inaccuracies and Inappropriate Content

As discussed in Section 2.2.3, rule-based chatbots reduce the risk of irrelevant or inappropriate conversation. No doubt for this reason, at their early stages of development, the developers of therapy bots Wysa and (the now defunct) Woebot expressly affirmed the value of rule-based approaches to chatbots in keeping the product within manageable guardrails. Indeed, the developers of the now defunct Woebot expressed the view that mental health is not 'ready for generative AI', noting the risks of misinformation, the erosion of trust and unsettling anthropomorphism (Darcy, 2023).[5] Nonetheless, rule-based chatbots can fail to provide contextually meaningful responses if the rules do not fit the scenario presented or if the chatbot cannot decode the initial prompt (White, 2018).

Chatbots relying on natural language processing models or generative AI present greater challenges of relevance, accuracy and safety. For example, Tay, a Microsoft chatbot on Twitter, was shut down in less

[5] Quote on file with author.

than twenty-four hours after learning to make racist and inflammatory statements (Lee, 2016). Gilbert et al. point to the risks arising from the combination of lack of context and generative AI's tendency to fabricate a plausible response to queries. They observe:

> [I]t is questionable whether their tendency to suggest harmful or false, yet highly plausible, information can ever be controlled .... In their current state, LLMs do not ask for missing information needed to provide an accurate answer, provide no accompanying indication of relative certainty or confidence, and generally provide no genuine sources (Gilbert et al., 2023: 2396).

In the context of mental health, the risk of unscripted conversation lies in the chatbot not only hallucinating content but also failing to recognise indicators of escalating ill-health or self-harm, or indeed, as alleged in recent litigation, encouraging such conduct (Duffy, 2024, 2025; Chatterjee, 2025). Nonetheless, as discussed in Section 2.2.3, the attractions of an adaptive conversational style have meant some therapy bots are utilising generative AI, albeit with safeguards of fine-tuning and guardrails.

Outside these safeguards, the tendency to sycophantic interactions, combined with the underlying reality that generative AI chatbots, like AI companions, do not have a basis in mental health support, makes it close to inevitable that they may prove insufficiently attentive to the mental health of the user. A study by Ben-Zion et al. found that emotion-inducing prompts can exacerbate bias and error in generative AI chatbots, which may work against the interests of their users (Ben-Zion et al., 2025). These are risks that no specialist AI mental health tool would wish to countenance. Any developer seeking to incorporate generative AI capabilities in a therapy bot should accordingly seek to implement strong safeguards against such responses, although the limitations of these approaches have possibly led to an overreliance on disclaimers (discussed in Section 3.4.2).

Lack of Transparency

The field of responsible AI, principles of AI transparency and explainability (interpretability) of AI perform a central role. These principles require sufficient information for users to understand how an AI tool produces its outputs. The demands may be satisfied by information about the LLM model underlying the tool, the data used for training and the guardrails imposed. It may be more granular as to how any particular output was reached, or at least the counterfactuals, that is, what change in the input would have produced a different output.

Not all consumers will be interested in transparency (Paterson, 2024). However, as argued by Frank Pasquale, rights to transparency and explanations provide an opportunity for consumers and their advocates to identify unlawful biases or other flaws in AI-informed decisions and hold the deploying firms to account (Pasquale, 2025). There is little transparency about the combinations of technologies used in therapy bots and other direct-to-consumer digital mental health support tools. Nor is there much by way of explicit concern about bias. Developers have shown some concern to improve the accuracy and reduce the risk of inappropriate responses.

3.3.2 Developer Responses to Misaligned or Inappropriate Outputs from Therapy Chatbots

The developers of therapy bots have, to some extent, aimed to embrace the adaptivity and responsiveness of AI, and impose some guardrails around the use of their tools. These safeguards primarily manifest as training for chatbots for expertise in mental health and warnings to consumers about the circumstances in which the tools should not be used.

Fine-Tuning

As indicated in Section 2.2.3, one way of managing the risk of hallucination is simply to rely on rule-based rather than generative AI chatbots. Other developers have been seeking to 'fine-tune' the LLMs underlying generative AI chatbots on smaller, more reliable datasets to improve accuracy in specialised domains, including for mental health support (Gilbert et al., 2023: 2397), as well as imposing guardrails against inappropriate responses.

Thus, Wysa has advised that 'we are now integrating Gen AI into Wysa, both to meet user needs and to demonstrate how the risks associated with this technology can be addressed responsibly' (Aggarwal, 2024). Headspace's Ebb is described as a 'conversational chatbot', with a 'proprietary safety system to identify and route members to additional care based on risks, such as suicidal ideation, self-harm, abuse, and more' (Headspace, Meet Ebb). Newer entrants 'Therabot' by Dartmouth College and 'Ash' by SlingshotAI use fine-tuned generative AI for mental health support, within appropriate guardrails, for a more conversational experience (Economist, 2025b).

While rule-based responses reduce harmful outputs, they do not remove the risk of misaligned responses that arise from a misunderstanding of the consumer's prompt. Similarly, while fine-tuning and guardrails may steer generative AI chatbots away from inappropriate content or advice, these protections may be avoided or simply prove ineffective, given the range of ways in which poor mental health may be manifested. Fine-tuning the chatbots for mental health support may further reduce their responsiveness to human prompts or their capacity to identify warning signs of self-harm or deteriorating mental health.

Warnings

A different kind of response by developers to concerns about the risk of misaligned or inappropriate responses from therapy bots, lies in warnings about the viable scope of use and kinds of uses that are not supported. A number of digital mental health tools, and, similarly, AI companions and general-purpose generative AI chatbots, recommend that they should not be used by consumers considering self-harm or experiencing mental illness.

For example:

> If you ever feel at risk of harming yourself or someone else, Ahead is not the right place to get crisis help. Please contact your local helpline immediately, or reach out to us so we can help connect you with support in your country (Ahead FAQ).

> Wysa is not designed to assist with crises such as abuse, severe mental health conditions that may cause feelings of suicide, harm to self, and any other medical emergencies. Wysa cannot and will not offer medical or clinical advice. It can only suggest that users seek advanced and professional medical help. Please reach out to your country-specific suicide hotline in case of an emergency (Wysa).

Some developers of general-purpose generative AI chatbots have responded to safety concerns by promising stricter guardrails on generative AI chatbots used for mental health, precluding suicide advice and providing referrals to helplines (OpenAI, 2025).

The purpose of these kinds of warnings, displayed on web pages and app interfaces, is to limit liability for harm (see Section 3.4.2) and (more charitably) to direct users in crisis to professional support. As discussed in Section 3.4.2, a similar response to this issue is now being mandated by some laws in the US for companion AI and generative AI chatbots. But warnings of this kind may not be effective to direct a consumer interacting with a chatbot to change their approach and seek specialist assistance if merely provided in the fine print of a landing or sign-up page.

To be more salient, warnings or limitations may need to be integrated into the chat interaction. The effectiveness even of this approach will depend on the sensitivity of the chatbot to the warning signs of self-harm and care in designing a response that does not itself traumatise the user. They require an ongoing commitment to oversight, testing and revising the approach. For example, do users notice, understand and act on the warnings or do they merely click past in their desire to keep interacting with the chatbot? Ultimately, there must be other options for users to obtain the mental health support they need to deal with the issues being disclaimed by the therapy bot.

3.3.3 Legal Responses to Concerns about AI Safety

The most direct response to concerns about harms arising from the use of AI in any kind of human-centred service is through laws specifically targeted at AI or designed to address AI digital safety. The criticism of these kinds of laws is that they may be insufficiently nuanced to the use of AI in particular domains. Thus, there have been some attempts in different jurisdictions to ban or impose restrictions on therapy bots and related direct-to-consumer digital mental health support tools, as well as on AI companions, also considered later. There is litigation against the developers of general-purpose generative AI chatbots, alleging negligence in the chatbots' responses to manifestations of poor mental health. For these kinds of legal interventions to be effective, they must be guided by clear objectives informed by an understanding of the relevant risks and the ways in which the tools are used, to which the discussion now turns.

Targeted AI Laws

The EU *AI Act* (2024), legislation aimed at AI developers and deployers, bans AI systems deploying 'subliminal' or 'purposefully manipulative or deceptive' techniques that have an objective or effect of 'materially distorting' a person's behaviour, and systems that exploit any of the 'vulnerabilities of a natural person' (Article 5). The Act also places demanding safety and efficacy style obligations for high-risk categories of AI, such as the use of AI to determine access to banking or education services, such as AI systems that are used for 'biometric classification' or 'emotional recognition' (Annex. III). These banned and high-risk categories might apply to some variations of AI companions but do not clearly extend to consumers using AI chatbots for personal or mental health support.

Other than in these categories, chatbots are classified as low risk and primarily subject to transparency requirements. Thus, Article 50 requires developers to 'ensure that AI systems intended to interact directly with natural persons are designed and developed in such a way that the natural persons concerned are informed that they are interacting with an AI system', unless this is apparent from the context.

Digital Safety Laws

Online safety is addressed by legislation in several jurisdictions, such as *Online Safety Acts* in Australia (2021) and the UK (2023), and the EU *Digital Services Act* (2022). Online safety legislation may be a response to concerns about children accessing sexually explicit or violent content via AI companions or general-purpose generative AI chatbots (BBC, 2025; FTC, 2025). The legislation allows regulators to demand safety features from developers of digital services, such as limiting access by children or moderating violent content (European Parliament, 2025, e-Safety, 2025; Ofcom, 2024). Online safety laws also require platforms to assess and respond to content-based risk in specified domains. The UK regulator has confirmed that safety expectations will apply to chatbots, especially in relation to child safety and the protection of women or girls (Ofcom, 2024). While important, these 'online safety'-style interventions do not capture the full suite of concerns about AI and mental health.

Restrictions and Bans

Bans and restrictions on sale are usually a last resort for regulatory regimes because they cut across the operation of the market and consumer choice. They may be imposed where a product or some of its features are considered too harmful to be allowed on the market or to be accessed without age-based protocols or specialist oversight. Some jurisdictions in the US have enacted laws banning or restricting the use of therapy bots or companion/general-purpose chatbots on mental health grounds.

Legislation in Illinois and Utah prohibits the use of AI in mental health support other than where it is overseen by a licensed professional responsible for the operation of the system and with consent from the patient (Illinois, 2025; Utah, 2025). In 2025 California prohibited companion chatbots from operating without a protocol for identifying indications of self-harm or suicidal ideation, and where used by young people, requiring reminders to take a break from the interaction (California, 2025). New legislation in New York follows a similar approach (New York, 2025). These kinds of intervention are a response to the alarming high-profile cases of self-harm or suicide arising from interactions with companion and general AI chatbots and tools promoting their mental health benefits without any involvement from mental health professionals (Griesser, 2025).

As the Californian example indicates, children are often considered worthy of special protections in interactions dealing with AI. In September 2025, the FTC announced an inquiry into the harmful effects of AI companion bots on children (FTC, 2025), while Australia's e-Safety Commissioner has imposed obligations on developers to prevent children accessing sexually explicit AI companions (e-Safety Commissioner, 2025). Restrictions on chatbots being accessed by children may be justified by reference to the limitations of these technologies in responding to children's unusual use of language and unique emotional needs (Kurian, 2025). However, bans provide little guidance to consumers, including those with low digital literacy, about the ways in which they might usefully select and engage with the tools that remain on the market, or AI chatbots more generally (cf. Black Dog Institute, 2025). Thus consumer-focused education and protection initiatives may also be required.

3.4 Consumer Protection

A fourth lens for assessing the risks of harm from therapy bots, and possible legal responses, is consumer protection. Given that therapy bots and other direct-to-consumer digital mental health support tools are provided for the purpose of supporting the well-being of consumers, consumer protection would seem to be a particularly relevant consideration overseeing their performance. These are far-reaching laws which apply even when a service is provided using AI (Paterson & Maker, 2024). Yet many popular therapy bots and other digital mental health support tools perform poorly on most consumer-facing measures (World Economic Forum and Deloitte, 2021: 18). Indeed, it may be that their quasi-medical status has distracted developers and regulators from consumer protection considerations.

This section considers the range of possibly relevant consumer protection considerations in assessing the possible risks and benefits of direct-to-consumer digital mental health tools and associated uses of companion AI and general-purpose generative AI chatbots. Before turning to these matters, however, it is worth considering the possibility that consumers themselves can effectively regulate the market offering through their use choices.

3.4.1 The Limits of Consumer Choice

It might be argued that provided there is accurate information about the various digital mental health tools and alternative offerings (as discussed in Section 3.3.3), then consumers should be left to choose for themselves whether to use the tools and what tools they will use. This approach might be suggested to have the merit of giving consumers agency in accessing the mental health support they prefer and that consumers' assessment of what is useful to them should not be second guessed by regulators or lawmakers. Certainly, in principle, respect for individual autonomy means allowing parties to select the services they desire and empowering them to enter into the contracts they choose on the terms they assess as suiting them best. This approach allows market mechanisms to reward the developers of useful products and permits parties to allocate risk in the manner they judge most efficient, with corresponding adjustments in price.

In reality, consumers of the services of therapy bots and other direct-to-consumer digital mental health support tools will usually be at a relative disadvantage in selecting a service suitable for their needs and preferences. Consumers are likely to be unfamiliar with the workings of the AI technologies being deployed and the contractual terms may differ drastically from the arrangements in place when dealing with a human mental health professional. The services of such tools are provided without the intervention or involvement of a professional who might otherwise guide consumers on how and when they should be used. Moreover, chatbot services are presumably being used by cohorts of consumers who are highly likely to be experiencing vulnerability, people concerned about their mental health, who may, during their use of the tool, face a mental health crisis.

Here, it might be suggested the answer is for consumers to seek reliable information about the tools suitable for their needs. However, finding this information is likely to prove difficult even for the narrower category of specifically designed therapy bots, as opposed to AI companions or general-purpose chatbots co-opted for this use. This difficulty arises because different and often inconsistent measures are used to promote and review them.

In their promotional materials, developers of therapy bots and related digital mental health support tools typically seek to establish the efficacy of their products in a number of ways. Once interrogated, these measures are less robust than they might at first appear. Importantly, these measures also focus on discrete features of the tools, making an overall assessment of the benefits and risks difficult.

Information about Performance

Some digital mental health support tools provide statistics quantifying the benefits to consumers who make regular use of them. For example:

> 84% of Calm users who used the app 5x a week saw an improvement in their mental health (Calm, Welcome to Calm).
>
> 10 days of Headspace resulted in 12% decrease in stress; 4 weeks of Headspace reduces burnout; Headspace improves sleep in just 7 days' (Headspace).
>
> Youper contributes to reducing symptoms of six different mental health conditions and has supported the well-being of over two million people (Youper, Effectiveness).

Such statistics might be interpreted as supplying robust scientific backing for the service being provided. However, it is not always clear how these statistics have been ascertained. Additionally, the terms of service for these tools commonly disclaim many of these promised benefits, as discussed in Section 4.1.1.

Testimonials

Another common form of promotion for therapy bots and other direct-to-consumer digital mental health support tools is testimonials from users reporting on the benefits provided by the service. For example, Sensa's home page states: 'Don't just take our word for it. Hear how Sensa has improved the lives of these users' (Sensa). Online reviews and testimonials may help consumers in choosing between traditional consumer products, although there have been concerns about traders manipulating the review process (Australian Competition and Consumer Commission, 2020).

User reviews may be less helpful with higher-stakes products. This is because the people leaving reviews or rankings may not reflect the demographics of the likely user group or their experiences. They do not reflect outcomes over a sustained, or even uniform, period. Neary and Schueller (2018: 532) have observed that 'people who rate apps might not have engaged with an app long enough to explore its full functionality and likely lack the necessary expertise to comment on aspects such as the inclusion of evidence-based strategies'.

Third-Party Rankings

Other digital mental health support tools list third-party rankings. Some rankings are from websites or online magazines. Some rankings are based on criteria that are opaque and even for which a commission is paid (see, e.g., Braun & Cronkleton, 2022). Other rankings are focused on non-technical or medical criteria such as 'experience' or 'usability' (see, e.g., Blackwell, 2023; Dorwart, 2025). The user interface is a significant criterion in assessing the success of an app, recognising that it must not unduly increase cognitive load (Chandrashekar, 2018: 2). However, this feature must be assessed against other considerations, such as privacy and efficacy, to provide meaningful guidance for consumers.

Some digital mental health tools promote the expertise of the developers. For example:

> Built by scientists trained at Universities of Oxford, Cambridge, and Harvard (Ahead).
>
> Flourish Science is built by mission-driven psychologists, scientists, designers, and technologists. (Flourish)

While having scientists or psychologists in the development team is undoubtedly desirable, their presence does not guarantee good technical performance or fair marketing practices.

Potentially useful are independent rankings from not-for-profit organisations with their own developed criteria, notably from Mozilla and One Mind PsyberGuide (see Neary & Schueller, 2018: 534–535). The difficulty for consumers is that these rankings prioritise different factors. Mozilla provides a ranking on privacy and security (Mozilla, 2022 and 2023). One Mind PsyberGuide rates available apps using four criteria: credibility, transparency, user experience and professional reviews (One Mind PsyberGuide). An app commended for a good privacy policy (Mozilla, 2022) or innovative use of technology (Asar, 2020) may not actually be effective in providing mental health support, or vice versa. For example, Headspace ranks well as a mindfulness app (One Mind PsyberGuide) but poorly in terms of privacy (Mozilla, 2022 and 2023). These kinds of rankings do not interrogate the scientific studies behind the claims or consider the fairness of the contract terms. These limitations of viable metrics make robust consumer protection especially important in the context of therapy bots.

3.4.2 The Role of Consumer Protection Law

Consumer protection law commonly operates through a combination of what is sometimes referred to as 'ex-ante' and 'ex-post' requirements. Ex-ante consumer protection laws impose safety standards and expectations that may apply before products enter the market and operate while they are in the market, with the aim of reducing the risk of harm. Ex-ante consumer protection in this context would lie in therapeutic goods regulation and online safety laws, discussed in Sections 3.1.2 and 3.3.3.

Ex-post regulation imposes liability for penalties and compensation where harm does occur. Ex-post regulation responds to instances of harm but should also provide incentives to businesses to exercise greater care in providing their services. Ex-post protections of this kind are found in common law actions for negligence and breach of contract. They are also found in legislation governing the supply of goods and services to consumers and enforced by regulatory agencies, such as Ofcom in the UK, the Australian Competition and Consumer Commission in Australia or the Federal Trade Commission ('FTC') in the US. Regulators are responsible for enforcing prescriptive conduct obligations, such as prohibitions on misleading, unfair or unconscionable conduct found in the US *Federal Trade Commission Act* (15 U.S.C. §§ 45(a)(1), 45(n)), the EU *Unfair Commercial Practices Directive* (Directive 2005/29/EC, art. 6, 2005 O. J. (L 149) 22, 28), UK *Consumer Protection from Unfair Trading Regulations 2008* regs 5–6 or the *Australian Consumer Law* ss 18 and 21. These core 'safety-net' protections are typically expressed as open-textured standards, which makes them capable of adapting to new manifestations of the prohibited conduct, including those raised by emerging technologies (Paterson & Maker, 2024). They certainly have an application in the domain of therapy bots and other direct-to-consumer digital mental health support tools, as well as to AI companions and general-purpose generative AI chatbots.

Misleading Promotional Claims

Most therapy bots and other direct-to-consumer digital mental health support tools, as well as some companion AI, make claims about contributing to good mental health or improving poor mental health. Sometimes this is expressed directly and other times it is expressed through references to symptoms of poor mental health such as stress, anxiety, sleeplessness or poor focus. The impression conveyed by the marketing or headline claims made by the developers of these tools is that they can improve consumers' mental health outcomes (Oppenheim, 2019). As discussed in Section 3.4.1, the marketing for direct-to-consumer digital mental health tools may also claim that there is scientific support for their effectiveness, which are often overstated by reference to published research. Furthermore, it is possible that claims to assist mental health outcomes that are not realised may in some instances make users' mental health worse.

The FTC has made numerous statements about the pitfalls of 'fake AI' and indicated that it will be vigilant in policing such claims (FTC, 2024), although there has been little action by regulators in ensuring the veracity of claims by developers of AI-services provided directly to consumers, including in mental health. Nonetheless, headline marketing may breach misleading under consumer protection or tort law. For example, a digital mental health support tool claiming proven beneficial outcomes or scientific backing for the product when the available published evidence is ambiguous, inconclusive or negative may be misleading contrary to law.

Prohibitions on misleading conduct may also respond to unfounded claims or statements by AI companions or general-purpose generative AI chatbots that make unwarranted claims about having expertise in mental health diagnosis or support. Potentially, even claims to empathy or care, when these are synthetic representations of such feelings expressed by a chatbot, may be misleading, especially where the expression of care is rooted in the objective of prolonging conversations (for a fee or other commercial gain), promoting products (through virtual product placement) or upselling the user to higher priced features (for an AI companion) (Paterson & Bant, 2026).

Duties of Care in Providing the Service

Developers (and deployers) of therapy bots and other direct-to-consumer digital mental health support tools will usually owe a duty of care in providing their services to consumers, which arises through the tort of negligence and statutory equivalents such as the *Consumer Rights Act 2015* (UK) s 49 or *Australian Consumer Law* s 61. At the time of writing, litigation, including for negligence, has been initiated by parents of young people who have committed suicide or self-harmed after sustained interactions with AI chatbots or companions (Booth, 2025; Duffy, 2024). The complaint is that developers failed to show reasonable care because the chatbots in question failed to recognise early indications of self-harm in users or even provided advice on suicide techniques (Lee, 2025). These risks have also been raised with respect to digital mental health tools (Srivastava, 2023).

For these cases to succeed, a plaintiff will need to show a causal connection between the developer's lack of care and the harm the plaintiff experienced after using the product. The causation question is fact dependent. On the breach of duty question, there is no lack of guidance on what reasonable care in providing an AI-informed service should require, given the global interest in AI safety and responsible AI standards, as discussed in Section 3.3. These standards suggest that the requisite level of care would certainly involve ongoing oversight and ongoing testing of the performance of the chatbot or other tool. Although there is little case law to date, failing to set reasonable guardrails on the content produced by an AI chatbot may also breach the developer's duty of care in making the product directly available to consumers.

Responses to Contractual Limitations

Some companies are seeking to defend the litigation against them on grounds of failing to respond appropriately or carefully to the mental health of their users by arguing that the uses in question were out of scope. The contractual terms for many direct-to-consumer therapy bots favour the interests of the provider, with a host of consumer-unfriendly terms that deny any responsibility or liability for the quality of the service provided. For example:

> The Headspace Entities are not responsible for the accuracy, reliability, effectiveness, or correct use of information you receive through or as generated by the products (Headspace, Terms and Conditions).
>
> The client remains 'solely responsible for evaluating and assessing his own health, including any need to seek appropriate guidance from a health care provider' (Sensa, General terms and Conditions).

The objective of these kinds of disclaimers and limitation clauses is to protect developers from liability for products that fail to deliver on their promises of improved health and well-being. But there seems to be a fundamental unfairness in attracting consumers with headline claims of effective and scientifically based mental health support, while simultaneously denying any responsibility to provide such a service. This kind of reliance on fine print terms to undermine consumer expectations and leverage information asymmetries is precisely the conduct that consumer protection law aims to address.

Parties are entitled to define the scope of the service they provide, but there is a point at which the disjunction between what is promised and what is provided becomes problematic (Paterson, 2026). Fine print exclusions of responsibility will not necessarily protect developers from liability if the headline claim is what is influencing consumers' reliance on the product. Some jurisdictions also oversee the validity of contractual limitations on the deployer's liability. In some jurisdictions, unfair terms regimes will render overreaching exclusions and limitations void, such as those in the UK *Consumer Rights Act* pt 2 and the *Australian Consumer Law* pt 2–3 (Paterson, 2026). Contractual restrictions on unfair contract terms are justified by the reality that consumers rarely have the expertise to assess the substance of the contracts they are offered or the safety of the products they may be seeking to buy. These issues affecting informed consumer decisions have been illustrated in the context of therapy bots in Section 3, demonstrating the difficulty of assessing and comparing the efficacy of the services being offered, let alone the terms on which they are offered.

4 Networked Regulation

The discussion so far has demonstrated that there are a number of laws that respond to many of the concerns about therapy bots and other direct-to-consumer digital mental health support tools. Although there is ongoing debate about whether and how AI should be regulated (Hacker et al., 2025), AI-specific laws are emerging in some jurisdictions. Therapy bots and other direct-to-consumer digital mental health tools are also subject to well-established legal regimes, covering therapeutic goods, privacy, duties of care and consumer transactions, and overseen by regulators. However, these various laws appear to have been underutilised in this context, meaning that their efficacy in the domain is largely untested.

As more attention is directed to concerns about the mental health effects of AI companions and general-purpose chatbots, the overall regulatory response remains fragmented and focused on specific restrictions (e.g., children) and new obligations on developers (e.g., warnings). This fragmented approach is unlikely to be effective given the rapidly evolving uses of AI for mental health support. Indeed, the solution to these concerns is unlikely to be found in any one law, current or future. Rather, the impact of therapy bots and related AI tools may most effectively be addressed by a response that is deliberately diverse and capable of adapting to the different features of the products, as well as their alternatives.

This section considers the limits of a siloed approach to regulation before turning to the possibility of a networked approach.

4.1 The Limits of Siloed Regulation

Responses to the risks of harm associated with therapy bots and other direct-to-consumer digital mental health support tools typically focus on the harms arising within different legal categories in isolation or 'silos', as illustrated in Figure 2. The siloed approach obscures both the cumulative burden of harm and the ways in which different kinds of laws might, in combination, produce stronger protections for consumers. The siloed approach also offers little capacity to adapt to rapid changes in the market or products. A siloed approach that fails to consider the operational relationships between different kinds of laws can have consequences for the overall effectiveness of the regulatory regime. It can encourage regulatory arbitrage on the part of developers or deployers of the products. It can produce regulatory inattention or a merely performative approach to regulation by policy-makers or regulators.

4.1.1 Regulatory Arbitrage

Regulatory arbitrage refers to the efforts of regulated entities to structure their products so that they fall, in form if not in substance, outside a regulated regime. As discussed in Section 3.1.2, to the extent that therapy bots and related direct-to-consumer digital mental health support tools are classed as lifestyle products or as merely applying established psychological therapies, they fall outside the scope of therapeutic goods regulation. Developers of these products appear to be using contractual terms and disclaimers to ensure their products avoid classification as therapeutic devices, which would subject them to additional scrutiny. As illustrated

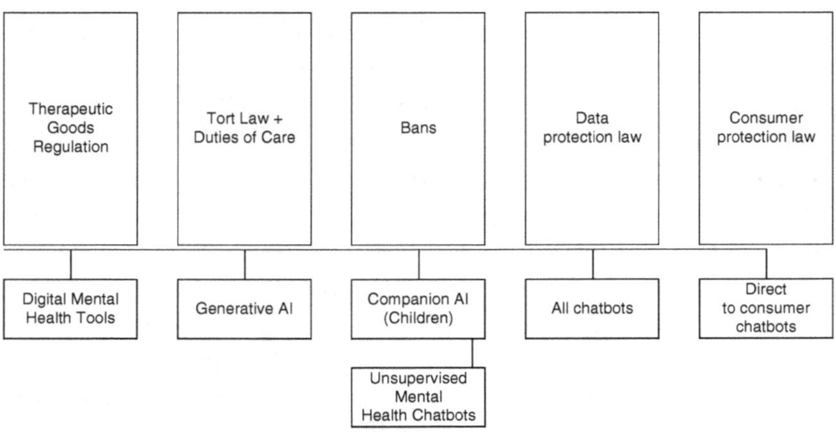

Figure 2 Regulatory silos for new technology

in Table 3, some developers of therapy bots are promoting their products using language that comes close to offering treatment for the symptoms of poor mental health, suggesting a therapeutic application. In most of these cases, the fine print terms of service of these chatbots expressly disclaim any therapeutic effect. The approach might be seen as mere caution or even respect for the complexity of mental health issues. However, the effect of these disclaimers is to take the chatbots outside the therapeutic goods regime and the robust oversight of outcomes that comes with the characterisation of a tool providing diagnosis or treatment.

There are several viable and available legal responses to the uncomfortable juxtaposition of these kinds of headline representations and contractual disclaimers. One response would focus on the headline claims used to promote a therapy bot and related tools in determining whether it falls within the scope of therapeutic goods regimes. On this approach, if the tool is promoted as having therapeutic effects, then it warrants regulation under that regime regardless of any disclaimer in the contractual terms. If the tool is genuinely not supportive of mental health in a therapeutic sense, it should not be described in terms that would be understood as suggesting otherwise.

Another response would be to focus on the inconsistency between the headline claims, to support mental health, and the fine print disclaimers, which deny this effect. A headline claim that is not supported by the substance of the product provided (as would be suggested by the extensive disclaimers) is misleading and should be sanctioned as such (via a regulatory strategy that has been used to respond to misleading privacy claims, discussed in Section 3.4.2).

Still another approach would focus on the care and skill required under tort and equivalent statutory regimes from the developers of direct-to-consumer mental health support tools and, similarly, companion AI or generative AI chatbots. If there are significant limitations to the efficacy of the product or it is critical that products not be used for crisis management or for diagnostic purposes, then this information is too important to be left to obscure fine print warnings, limitations or exclusion clauses. The information should be drawn to the attention of consumers in ways that are likely to be salient for their decision-making. Failing to do so should be treated as a failure of reasonable care, as it would likely influence consumers to make decisions they would not otherwise have made.

The broader point is that the effective regulation of therapy bots and other direct-to-consumer digital mental health tools, should not depend solely on whether the product is classed as inside or outside the therapeutic

Table 3 Contrast between marketing statements and limitations in terms of use for therapy bots

Tool	Marketing statement	Terms of Use
Flourish	'Feeling anxious? Stuck in critical self-talk? Sunnie is here to help. Sunnie is the world's first proactive mental health buddy' (Flourish)	'Flourish is not a medical or clinical service and does not provide diagnosis, treatment, or therapy for any mental health condition. The Services are intended for general well-being support and self-guided personal development and are not a substitute for professional mental health care. If you have any questions regarding your health or mental condition or behaviour, consult with a qualified professional' (Flourish, Terms and Conditions)
Headspace	'Feel less anxious with Headspace' (Headspace)	'While there is third-party evidence from research that meditation can assist in the prevention and recovery process for a wide array of conditions as well as in improving some performance and relationship issues, Headspace makes no claims, representations or guarantees that the Products provide a physical or therapeutic benefit.' (Headspace, Terms and Conditions)
Headspace (Ebb)	Ebb, has been trained to recognise and respond to risks 'such as suicidal ideation, self-harm, abuse, and more' (Headspace)	As above
Youper	The groundwork of Youper is evidence-based interventions, treatments that have been studied extensively and proven successful. Youper has been proven clinically effective at reducing symptoms of anxiety and depression by researchers at Stanford University' (Youper)	Youper will not 'assume any liability for inaccuracies or error in its content or representations' (Youper, Terms of Use)
Replika	'Build better habits and reduce anxiety' (Replika)	Replika can assist in the recovery process for a wide array of conditions, Replika makes no claims, representations or guarantees that the Services provide a therapeutic benefit' (Replika, Terms and Conditions)

goods regime. Rather, the relevant regulatory regime should be understood as encompassing the entire body of laws that combine to promote good outcomes for consumers. This approach demands regulatory coordination and reduces the risk of ineffective or 'performative' regulation.

4.1.2 Regulatory Inattention

The strength of therapeutic goods regimes lies in providing 'entry-level' scrutiny of medical devices (Carpenter, 2010: 164–165), which requires the operation of the product to have been validated and subject to ongoing monitoring. This kind of robust entry-level regulation aims to weed out harmful or poorly performing products and support health consumer and practitioner choice (Carpenter, 2010: 189; Shuren et al., 2018: 337). However, consumers using therapy bots outside the therapeutic goods regime still have protections under other laws, such as AI-targeted laws, data protection laws, consumer protection laws and the general laws of tort and contract.

These other kinds of laws have been used to support the objectives of the therapeutic goods regimes, for example, by ensuring that developers of products have a proper basis for any claims made about the products' benefits. For example, the FTC has relied on its jurisdiction over misleading conduct to regulate marketing claims about health-related products:

> Under FTC law, companies must back up claims about what their product can do with reliable evidence. If a company makes a claim about the health or safety benefits of a product, that claim must be based on scientific evidence. If a company claims that its product can cure, mitigate, or treat a serious disease such as cancer or heart disease, it must back up that claim through the accepted standards of scientific testing (FTC 2023a).

A similar approach could be taken to therapy bots that claim to be beneficial for mental health without verifying those claims by reference to research that withstands scientific scrutiny or disclaims effectiveness in the contractual terms of service. Currently, the consumer protection regulators in the UK (Ofcom), US (FTC) and Australia (ACCC) have yet to consider the consumer protection aspects of therapy bots and other direct-to-consumer digital mental health tools. This is the case even though the marketing for such products, and the contractual terms, uses the kinds of practices that have been subject to criticism and sanction in more traditional consumer markets.

It may be that the lack of regulatory attention given to therapy bots and other direct-to-consumer digital mental health tools arises from the combination of the optimistic promotion of the services offered by the chatbots and belief in the capacity of AI to supplement human services. In a climate where there are concerns about mental health and not enough support for people experiencing poor mental health or mental illness, optimism about the potential of therapy bots and other direct-to-consumer AI mental health tools has proved persuasive. In this light, regulators may simply have not considered that the products present sufficient risk to warrant closer examination.

Moreover, as noted in Section 3.1.2, the headline marketing for the services provided by therapy bots, although invoking mental health, avoids a direct reference to mental illness, which would squarely fall within therapeutic regimes. The products therefore sit at the boundaries of different regulatory schemes and this may account for them not squarely having been the focus of any one regulator. Lisa Parker et al. (2019b: 171) argue that '[d]ifferent aspects of a single [mental health support tool] may come under the jurisdiction of multiple upstream regulators, with none of them appearing to take overall responsibility for the product' (Parker et al., 2019b). The lack of any sustained regulatory scrutiny of direct-to-consumer therapy bots may also reflect the impact of discipline, not just regulatory, silos.

Studies on therapy bots and other direct-to-consumer digital mental health support tools have tended to focus on discrete issues, such as the effectiveness of the therapy offered or the level of privacy protection provided, as opposed to a more holistic assessment. This absence of formal regulatory attention means other forces, such as those arising from funding and market opportunities, will influence the way in which the products are developed and deployed. As Christine Parker et al. point out:

> Even when official government policy leaves contentious issues to the market, this does not leave the issue un-regulated. Rather there are always networks of public and private actors who influence and regulate market conduct more or less directly, and more or less effectively or legitimately, regardless of whether government has designed and implemented specific regulatory policy or not (Parker et al., 2017: 369).

To date, regulators, and health industry bodies, have missed opportunities to design effective regulatory responses to the risks of direct-to-consumer digital mental health chatbots that would operate as market gatekeepers, reward best practices and sanction harmful ones. In the resulting vacuum, developers have sought to control the narrative, positioning their products as innocuous and essential, in the sense of filling an unmet demand for individualised mental health support.

The combined effect of how the chatbots are promoted and their aspiration to 'helpfulness' is regulatory inattention, a pattern observable in other fields as well. Chatbots are being deployed in government, law, finance and retail services (Paterson, 2025). In these areas, too, the dominant narrative is on assisting users and promoting efficiency. The many concerns arising from these uses, such as error, bias and data protection, are addressed individually if at all, rather than by reference to their cumulative impact. There are failings here of regulatory co-ordination, which also lead to reactive responses when things do go wrong.

4.1.3 Reactive Regulation

Growing concerns about the risks to consumers in relying on AI companions or general-purpose generative AI for mental health support have prompted some regulatory intervention. As discussed in Section 3.3.3, there are moves in some jurisdictions to provide greater protection for children through age-based limits on access and reminders to take a break. Additionally, California and New York have prohibited companion chatbots from operating without a protocol for identifying indications of self-harm or suicidal ideation (California, 2025; New York, 2025).

These might prove useful interventions. However, the initiatives have not precipitated a broader discussion about the need for more readily available mental health support nor how it should be provided. It is possible, therefore, that these kinds of response to the mental health harms of companion AI and general-purpose generative AI chatbots may be more reactive than effective. Put starkly, requiring chatbot developers to identify signs of ill health and refer those consumers to mental health support services may be technically unrealistic and practically unhelpful. Referrals to support lines provide little relief to those with poor mental health if the support services are underfunded and oversubscribed (Stokel-Walker, 2025). And there is no evidence that a referral or reminder to take a break provides an effective prompt to a consumer to change their habits when they are enamoured with their AI companion or feel they have no other forms of social support.

4.2 The Way Forward?

The increasing availability of therapy bots and other direct-to-consumer digital mental health support tools may shape the market for mental health support services, pushing the norm towards automation rather than increased funding for human therapists. Pasquale questions 'whether the tools are prematurely disrupting markets for (and the profession of) mental health care to accelerate the substitution of cheap (if limited) software for more expensive, expert, and empathetic professionals' (Pasquale, 2019). These observations underlie the potential for therapy bots to be a potent case study for Zuboff's 'surveillance capitalism', which describes the commodification of individual experiences and behaviours via extensive data processing (Zuboff, 2019).

It is also possible that this trajectory, towards the commodification of mental health services, has already been disrupted. And that the disruption comes from another form of automation, namely consumers' reliance on companion AI and general-purpose generative AI. The fact that these more general offerings may provide worse health outcomes or have minimal efficacy in achieving positive outcomes is not necessarily a reason to turn back to specialised therapy bots and other digital mental health support tools. But concerns about harmful interactions between consumers and general-purpose generative AI chatbots, may make more attractive the possibility of digital mental health support tools carefully built by professionals with domain expertise, in collaboration with people with profound lived experience, and then comprehensively tested. Or it might drain interest and investment out of that more specialised market altogether.

Whichever future is envisaged, well-designed and implemented regulatory regimes can play a role in curtailing harm and providing incentives to safer and more suitable products. However, more nuance is needed in how we think about the structure and role of effective regulation. In considering the harms introduced by new technology, there appears to be an inclination to find one response that will resolve the concerns. This search for the one 'right law' is understandable given the magnitude of the task. However, as the previous sections have demonstrated, the affordances of therapy bots and related offerings vary considerably across different sectors. These features may mean embracing more complexity and diversity in the relevant regulatory response and approach that might be conceived as relying on *distributed regulatory networks*. However, first it is necessary to consider the concern about the impact of this approach on the drive to innovate.

4.2.1 Innovation and the 'Cost' of Regulation

A common objection to new laws applying to AI, or new ways of applying existing laws, is that such initiatives will stifle innovation (Productivity Commission, 2025). The concern is that more focused and expansive regulation will impede the development of useful applications of the technology, such as genuinely beneficial therapy bots and other digital mental health support tools. The characterisation of innovation and regulation as being mutually exclusive has been criticised (Paterson, 2026) and has certainly not been established. It is entirely plausible that using the suite of effectively targeted laws to promote best practice will lead to more innovative outcomes benefiting consumers. Equally, uneven enforcement of existing law may favour non-conforming or poorer quality services: the proverbial race to the bottom.

An illustration of this paradigm is found in the withdrawal of Woebot from the market in July 2025. Woebot was a mental health support chatbot using cognitive behavioural therapy (see Table 1). The developers of Woebot stated that the reasons for its withdrawal from the market lay in the challenge of meeting the FDA's requirements for using large language models to provide mental health support and a lack of clarity about those requirements (Stat News, 2025). It may be that the service provided by Woebot required too much oversight or was too rigid to be viable as a stand-alone commercial product. However, if we take the developers' statement at face value, the outcome may be seen as a perverse consequence of an overly reactive approach to the use of chatbots for mental health support. Woebot was regarded by some commentators as one of the better products available to consumers (Wallace, 2025b). Woebot used a rules-based approach in its chatbot to constrain the risk of inappropriate responses (Darcy, 2023). Woebot was rated as being privacy-preserving by Mozilla (2023) and providing a good user experience by One Mind PsyberGuide (n.d.). Woebot was built and operated by psychologists undertaking clinical research on the performance of the product (Darcy et al., 2021).

The current approach to regulating direct-to-consumer digital mental health tools arguably favours those products that are designed to navigate around the boundaries of therapeutic goods regulation. It may also leave the ground open for generative AI offerings that do not purport to support mental health but may nonetheless be used in this way despite having no expertise and a propensity to inept responses (Wallace, 2025a). By contrast, a more holistic understanding of the way in which existing laws, and other market interventions, respond to the harmful manifestations of AI therapy bots – distributed, networked regulation – might support a level playing field for the development of more robustly validated, tested and refined approaches to digital mental health support.

4.2.2 Regulatory Networks

While the nuances of relevant laws may vary between jurisdictions, the underlying demand for the regulation of products being offered to consumers is relatively straightforward. State-of-the-art technology should not divert attention from the misuse of practices that are known to erode consumer welfare in other contexts. Lifestyle products should deliver safe and welfare-enhancing outcomes consistent with their headline representations. Health-related products should be safe for their promoted and foreseeable uses. Data should not be extracted and used against consumers or in ways that are contrary to their reasonable expectations. Contractual rights and limitations should be balanced, consistent with headline marketing and salient to consumer users.

The challenge lies in co-ordinating the various regulators that may be involved in ensuring these outcomes, given that the products that may make claims to mental health support are situated across several fields of regulation and invoke the expertise of mental health professionals and the lived experience of those who use the technology. In this context, there is no one law or lead regulator who can resolve concerns about the risks associated with the support services being offered. Instead, there is a network of market participants, who have the capacity to influence the ways in which the services are delivered and the quality of what is provided.

This picture of multiple influences and modes of intervention might be seen as haphazard or dysfunctional. However, it reflects the reality of regulation in the kind of dynamic market presented by direct-to-consumer digital mental health support tools. Part of the complexity arises from the way in which the products themselves are presented and marketed. Additionally, regulating complex products in heterogeneous markets is inevitably multifaceted; this is all the more so when the purpose of the product is human well-being.

Christine Parker et al. argue that analyses and suggestions for regulatory interventions often assume that regulation is a unitary tool affecting relatively stable markets. Instead, they point to the insights available from a regulatory network analysis (Parker et al., 2017). Regulatory network analysis suggests that 'we should consider markets … as a set of changing relations in which public and private standards are continually being created, adjusted, solidified, or destroyed' (Parker et al., 2017: 370; also Braithwaite, 2006: 885). This insight allows recognition that changes to industry behaviour may most effectively be produced by acknowledging and co-ordinating the network of laws, regulators and other participants, that have the capacity to influence behaviour in the market in question. It also provides an opportunity for regulators, professional organisations and civil society groups with shared objectives to collaborate in shaping and promoting the kinds of market outcomes that genuinely benefit society. Applied to therapy bots and other direct-to-consumer digital mental health support tools, a regulatory network analysis means acknowledging the role of developers, tech companies, medical associations and consumer groups in shaping the affordances of the products being offered.

Network regulatory analysis means recognising that the law is not the only or even the most significant influence on outcomes in the regulated space. Rather 'the state becomes part of a network of regulation in which the tasks of regulation are redistributed in various ways among actors within the network' (Drahos & Krygier, 2016: 3). Within the apparatus of the state, however, there is a network of regulation in which tasks are distributed between laws and regulators. In other words, there is a sense in which the legal regime itself operates as a regulatory network and the success of regulatory objectives is reliant on a network of cognate interrelated laws (Figure 3).

A regulatory network analysis recognises that a product's features may enliven numerous laws and that more than one regime may offer

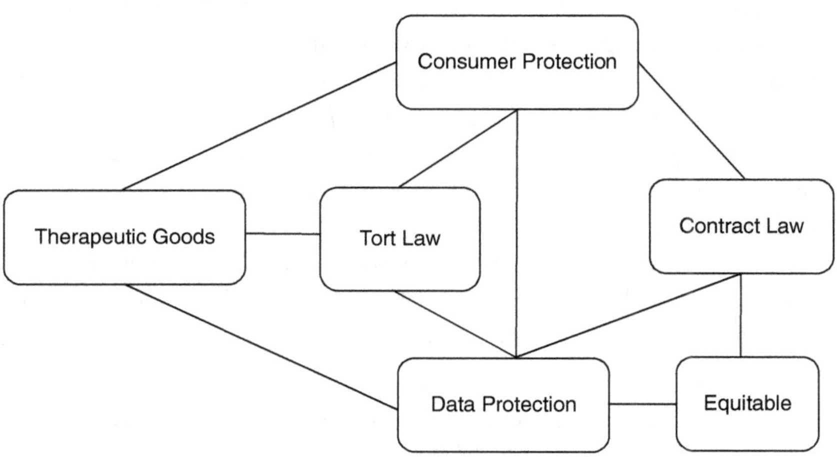

Figure 3 Legal networks

a valid response to concerns about the efficacy or safety of that product. The requirements for testing and oversight provided by therapeutic goods regulations set a basis for safer, more effective products but need to be supplemented by consumer protection oversight, ensuring that contracting practices are not misleading or otherwise overreaching. To the extent that some products fall outside therapeutic goods regulation, consumer protection laws need to be rigorously enforced. Regulators should be particularly vigilant in the case of products using new forms of AI, especially generative AI, given the associated risks of bias and inaccuracy. The approach requires co-ordination and also a degree of dynamism as the risks and challenges evolve with different iterations of the available products as frequently as every six months (Torous & Rodriguez-Villa, 2021).

Stakeholders other than regulators have a role in promoting a greater level of safety and reliability in therapy bots and other direct-to-consumer digital mental health support tools. The work of regulators might be complemented by cross-industry standards or guidelines which reduce the work that needs to be done by individuals in assessing standardised features of mental health chatbots, such as privacy and security (Australian Commission on Safety and Quality in Health Care, 2020). Work has already been done on developing guidelines and standards for digital mental health support tools (World Economic Forum and Deloitte White Paper, 2022: 12–15; Neary and Schueller, 2018: 533–534). Australia has implemented standards and a voluntary accreditation scheme for digital mental health products to address key safety and quality concerns (Australian Commission on Safety and Quality in Health Care, 2020; see also, Steindl, 2023).[6] The Mental Health Commission of Canada (2023) has developed a National Assessment Framework for e-Mental Health support tools based on standards covering data and privacy; clinical evidence; clinical safety; usability and accessibility; security and technical stability; cultural safety, social responsibility and equity; and enhanced data sovereignty. The World Economic Forum with Deloitte (World Economic Forum, 2021) has also developed a framework for governance of digital mental health support tools.

Critically, there needs to be consensus on the content, design and implementation of such guidelines and standards, as well as an authoritative means of verifying compliance (Fraser et al., 2024). As Henry Fraser et al.

[6] The standards are not intended to apply to more generic wellness service (Australian Commission on Safety and Quality in Health Care, 2020: 4).

explain, 'standards tend to work best, and carry the greatest imprimatur of legitimacy, when there is consensus about goals and at least some degree of agreement and clarity about practical implementation' (Fraser et al., 2024: 112). A stronger mechanism for achieving consensus could involve external expert certification (cf. Fraser et al., 2024: 116) and a system for signalling rankings to mental health professionals and consumers, possibly through a star system or trust mark (Neary & Schueller, 2018: 534–535). Neary and Schueller (2018: 534) also argue that '[m]ultidimensional ratings are useful for consumers and clinicians because some characteristics might be more important for different people or purposes'. Additionally, there should be stakeholder education about the role and scope of the guidelines or standards.

Another site of regulation lies with mental health professionals and their professional associations. Professional associations have a role in guiding developers and educating members about their operations. For example, the American Psychiatric Association has developed a five-stage app rating model for clinicians based on a series of questions to investigate across five fields: access and background; privacy and safety; clinical foundation; usability; and therapeutic goal (American Psychiatric Association, n.d.). This kind of approach is useful in its focus on the needs of patients and treating psychiatrists. Mental health services in Australia have provided guidance to consumers on choosing a digital mental health product, and the limitations of more general generative AI chatbots (Beyond Blue; Black Dog Institute).

The capacity of intermediaries in the market for therapy bots and other direct-to-consumer digital mental health support tools to hold developers to appropriate standards of performance should be recognised and utilised. App stores should be responsible for removing products that misrepresent their scope, or which make claims that are entirely unverified (Mattioli, 2021: 34). For developers of therapy bots that want to comply with best practice, there are guidelines, standards and assurance frameworks developed in conjunction with industry, professionals and users that can assist. Verified compliance with these standards is a way of signalling trustworthiness by developers of digital mental health support tools and a way for health professionals to be secure in recommending the products to clients. Compliance with standards can also be a necessary (but not conclusive) indication that a service provider has exercised reasonable care in improving the service as required under tort and some statute law.

4.2.3 Distributed Regulation

While existing systems of regulation can be understood as working most effectively as networks of influence, the debate around regulating products or services involving AI often focuses on the need for 'a' law responding to the harms of the technology. Given the rapidly changing capacity of the technology and the multiple touchpoints for harm, laws might better be conceived as distributed across multiple nodes. This means recognising more than one site of response for different kinds of harm or risk. Without centralising responsibility in any one agency, regulatory responsibility is distributed across participants in the network, promoting those with the best capacity to promote any particular regulatory objective in their relevant sphere of operation that is relevant in the context at any point in time.

The need for different legal nodes responding to AI harms need not represent a failure in the system. Rather, it is a sign of adaptivity: it means the legal regime as a whole contains multiple sites for refining and reframing the characterisation of rights and responsibilities for addressing new technologies or other developments in the market (Figure 4).

For example, as discussed earlier, the risks to consumers from data processing may be addressed by a combination of data protection law requirements for notice, consent and conduct-style duties applying to data processing, consumer law prohibitions on misleading conduct, privacy torts, breach of confidence or even the development of fiduciary-like duties for those who hold sensitive information (on the latter, see Dove et al., 2026). The FTC has signalled a preparedness to use its regulatory powers to address concerns about bias and unfairness in consumer AI applications

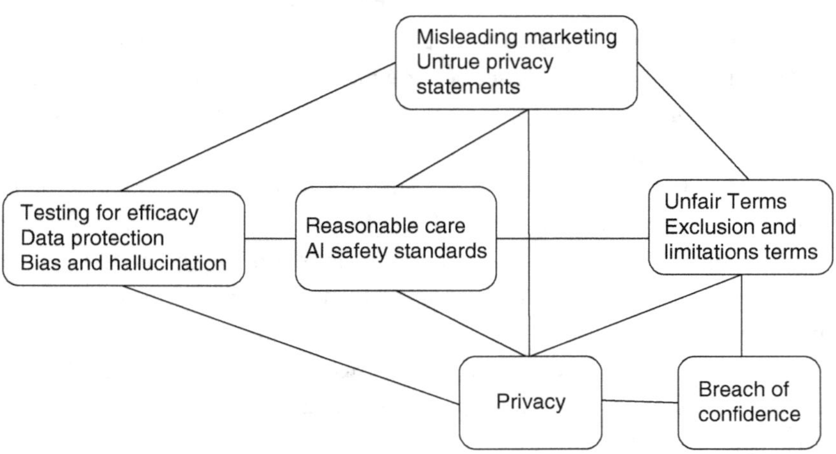

Figure 4 Distributed (legal) regulation

(Jillson, 2021; Australian Competition and Consumer Commission, 2019; Innovation, Science and Economic Development Canada, n.d.; Competition and Markets Authority, 2020). Contractual limitations may be tackled as unfair or misleading terms, or circumvented as irrelevant for the purposes of therapeutic goods characterisation of products for which the headline advertising promotes a mental health response (Medicines & Healthcare Products Regulatory Agency, 2025).

More effective regulatory responses to the harms that may be occasioned by therapy bots and other direct-to-consumer digital mental health tools do not necessarily ensure the ongoing viability or efficacy of these products. Consumers may continue to prefer AI companions or general-purpose generative AI chatbots over specialised therapy bots. Rule-based therapy bots may be more secure but linguistically limited and more conversationally adept generative AI therapy bots may still not be engaging as an AI companion. Health professionals may develop new kinds of products or use instead AI to improve the efficiency of administrative processes, giving them more time for clients. However, greater recognition of the role of distributed regulatory networks may address the more overtly harmful aspects of direct-to-consumer digital mental health tools and also improve their overall performance in the eyes of consumers.

Regulatory initiatives focused on specifically designed digital mental health tools still leave the risks of harms from companion AI or general-purpose generative AI chatbots to be resolved. But similar lessons can apply to these offerings as well. Moreover, a more effective regulatory stance on therapy bots may create space for a more deliberate and informed discussion about the place for these other kinds of AI chatbots, and their influence on the mental health of the humans who interact with them.

Conclusion

From Eliza to Wysa, the possibility of chatbots providing mental health support has remained a preoccupation of developers and researchers. For many, therapy bots represent an alluring technological advance and a useful response to the unmet need for mental health support. However, as this Element has discussed, despite numerous online offerings, the overall benefits of specifically designed therapy bots and other direct-to-consumer digital mental health support tools remain uncertain. The therapeutic effect of these products has yet to be established, especially for already marginalised cohorts (Section 3.1). The data practices of many developers of direct-to-consumer digital mental health tools are unclear and possibly inconsistent with user expectations (Section 3.2). It does not appear that the tools are tested for fairness (or lack of bias), equity or accessibility (Section 3.3). Exclusion and limitation of liability clauses found in the fine-print terms of service for therapy bots and other digital mental health support tools commonly disclaim responsibility for improved mental health outcomes, including the outcomes used to market the products in the first place (Section 3.4). Developers routinely promote these products' capacity for mental health support but advise against their use during mental health crises and illness, thereby avoiding the more robust regulatory regime that applies to therapeutic goods (Section 4.1.1).

Even if the individual harms arising from therapy bots and other direct-to-consumer digital mental health tools seem insignificant, cumulatively they may be highly impactful. Therapy bots tinker with our minds, and those who seek to use them deserve the respect of a carefully designed and tested product, accompanied by ongoing robust systems and processes for governance. Decisions about where to invest resources by governments, health services and consumers should be based on a realistic understanding of the performance of the products and the best use of AI in the mental health context (Blease & Torous, 2023). It is possible that therapy bots and other digital mental health support tools work best when embedded in clinical practice which would oversee their interactions with mental health consumers.

Regardless of where these debates land, specifically designed therapy bots are being overtaken by less specialised offerings, in the form of AI companions and general-purpose generative AI chatbots. At least to users, these offerings may appear to offer equivalent services in a more engaging and interactive manner. They may also come with higher risks of serious mental health harms than specifically designed digital mental health tools. Examples of user self-harm following interactions with companion AI and emerging research on the sycophantic tendencies of general-purpose generative AI chatbots suggest that they may ultimately be harmful to mental health (see Section 2.2.2). However, just as specifically designed therapy bots and other direct-to-consumer digital mental health support tools may divert resources from human-centred services, 'free' general-purpose generative AI may divert them from more specialised offerings without delivering a clear benefit to users. Again, a clear understanding of the risks and benefits the products offer is imperative, as are well-targeted responses to unacceptable levels of risk.

An effective regulatory response to concerns about the risks of harm from AI products deployed for use by consumers is more complex than simply enacting a new law or activating an existing legal regime in a particular domain. This Element has suggested that realising this ambition means understanding the applicable laws as forming part of a regulatory network, which operates in conjunction with other influences on regulatory objectives, and the distributed nature of those laws in supporting effective regulation. This approach does not make the regulatory regime incoherent, nor does it amount to over-regulation. Rather, it recognises the different affordances of direct-to-consumer digital mental health support tools and the impact of services that can be repurposed by consumers for a similar function.

The lessons to be drawn from this analysis are not limited to laws responding to the risk of harm from therapy bots, AI companions or general-purpose generative AI chatbots used for mental health support. There are insights for AI regulation more generally. There is a tendency in calls for stronger regulation of new AI-based products to demand new laws rather than activate those that already exist. There may be ways in which existing laws do not adequately address, or be proactive in reducing, the harms of AI in ways that are effective or fair. However, any AI law is unlikely to be comprehensive and will need to operate in conjunction with other kinds of laws, social policies and technological standards (Meese & Tan, 2026). Without attention to these interactions, existing and future, general and specific AI-directed laws may fail to achieve their intended purpose.

There are more fundamental considerations as well. The automation of mental health support and the growing use of general-purpose generative AI or companions for mental health require us to confront important questions of policy and values in human interactions with technology. The relational and equity consequences of the outsourcing of fundamental human services, and relationships, should be recognised and debated (Achtyes et al., 2023; Khawaja & Bélisle-Pipon, 2023). After having developed the therapeutic chat functions of Eliza, Weizenbaum asked whether 'we really believe that it helps people living in our already overly machine-like world to prefer therapy administered by machines to that given by other people' (Weizenbaum, 1976: 269)? We may have to ask whether humans really want to respond to loneliness and an absence of meaningful human companionship with an artificial entity, however initially alluring. Certainly, genuine collaboration between the various stakeholders – including people with lived experience of poor mental health, mental health professionals, computer scientists, developers, policy experts and regulators – is now more crucial than ever before.

References

7 Cups: www.7cups.com/ (accessed 14 July 2025), archived at https://perma.cc/G53M-TENN.

Achtyes, E. D., Glenn, T., Monteith, S., et al. (2023). Telepsychiatry in an Era of AI Mental Health Startups. *Current Psychiatry Reports*, 25(6), 263–272.

Adamopoulou, E. & Moussiades, L. (2020). Chatbots: History, Technology, and Applications. *Machine Learning with Applications*, 2, 100006.

Adams, J., Davies, J., Wattanatakulchat, P., Galante J., Miller F., D'Alfonso S., & Van Dam, N. T. (2026). Engagement with Meditation Apps: Cross-Sectional Survey of Use and Associations. *Journal of Medical Internet Research*, 28, e71960.

Aggarwal, J. (2024). *Responsible (Generative) AI for Mental Health: A Playbook* www.linkedin.com/pulse/responsible-generative-ai-mental-health-playbook-jo-aggarwal-itwbf/?trackingId=ynpc52tGB35o%2Fxl%2FVI1wKw%3D%3D.

aHead: www.ahead-app.com/ (accessed 16 October 2025), archived at https://perma.cc/VWS3-25JA.

aHead FAQ: www.ahead-app.com/ahead-faq (accessed 16 October 2025), archived at https://perma.cc/5TED-2ENU.

Aiyer, B., Bucaille, A., & Westcott, K. (2021). *Mental Health Goes Mobile: The Mental Health App Market Will Keep on Growing*, www.deloitte.com/us/en/insights/industry/technology/technology-media-and-telecom-predictions/2022/mental-health-app-market.html.

American Psychiatric Association. (n.d.). *The App Evaluation Model*, www.psychiatry.org/psychiatrists/practice/mental-health-apps/the-app-evaluation-model.

American Psychological Association. (2025). *Using Generic AI Chatbots for Mental Health Support: A Dangerous Trend.* www.apaservices.org/practice/business/technology/artificial-intelligence-chatbots-therapists.

Ananthapadmanaban, S. M., & Paterson, J. M. (2023). *Privacy and Consumer Protection Practices of Automated Mental Health, Wellbeing and Mindfulness Apps Report.* www.unimelb.edu.au/caide/research-archive/data-privacy-and-consumer-protection-practices-of-automated-mental-health,-wellbeing-and-mindfulness-apps.

Ananthapadmanaban, S. M., & Paterson, J. M. (2026). Can the UK, Australia, and India Master the Defence Against Dark Patterns? A Comparative Study of Jurisdictional Approaches. *Indian Journal of Law and Technology*, 21, 1.

Apple Health App: https://support.apple.com/en-au/105000 (accessed 8 July 2025), archived at https://perma.cc/3E8G-RZXB.

Ash: https://apps.apple.com/au/app/ash-ai-for-mental-health/id6474862947, archived at https://perma.cc/E74D-4T4E.

Asar, A. (2020). *Five Tech Innovations That Changed Mental Health in 2020*, www.forbes.com/sites/forbestechcouncil/2020/11/25/five-tech-innovations-that-changed-mental-health-in-2020/?sh=744f74f21e9c.

Atillah, I. E. (2023). *Man Ends His Life After an AI Chatbot 'Encouraged' Him to Sacrifice Himself to Stop Climate* Change, www.euronews.com/next/2023/03/31/man-ends-his-life-after-an-ai-chatbot-encouraged-him-to-sacrifice-himself-to-stop-climate-.

Australian Commission on Safety and Quality in Health Care. (2020). *National Safety and Quality Digital Mental Health Standards*.

Australian Competition and Consumer Commission. (2019). *Digital Platforms Inquiry: Final Report*. www.accc.gov.au/about-us/publications/serial-publications/digital-platform-services-inquiry-2020-25-reports/digital-platform-services-inquiry-final-report-march-2025.

Australian Competition and Consumer Commission. (2020). *HealthEngine to Pay $2.9 Million for Misleading Reviews and Patient Referrals* (Australia), www.accc.gov.au/media-release/healthengine-to-pay-29-million-for-misleading-reviews-and-patient-referrals.

Balcombe, L. (2026). Digital Mental Health Post COVID-19: The Era of AI Chatbots. *Encyclopedia*, 6(2), 32. https://doi.org/10.3390/encyclopedia6020032.

Barocas, S., & Selbst, A. D. (2016). Big Data's Disparate Impact. *California Law Review*, 104, 671–732.

Baumel, A., Muench, F., Edan, S., & Kane, J. M. (2019). Objective User Engagement with Mental Health Apps: Systematic Search and Panel-Based Usage Analysis. *Journal of Medical Internet Research*, 21(9), e14567.

BBC. (2025). *Character AI to Ban Teens from Talking to Its AI Chatbots*. www.bbc.com/news/articles/cq837y3v9y1o.

Bearable: https://bearable.app (accessed 8 July 2025), archived at https://perma.cc/TJ4Y-NEA3.

Bennike, I. H., Wieghorst, A., & Kirk, U. (2017). Online-Based Mindfulness Training Reduces Behavioral Markers of Mind Wandering. *Journal of Cognitive Enhancement*, 1, 172.

Ben-Zion, Z., Witte, K., Jagadish, A. K., et al. (2025). Assessing and Alleviating State Anxiety in Large Language Chatbots. *npj Digital Medicine*, 8, 132.

Bernardi, J. (2025). Friends for Sale: The Rise and Risks of AI Companions. *Ada Lovelace Institute*, Blog Post. www.adalovelaceinstitute.org/blog/ai-companions/.

BetterHelp: www.betterhelp.com/ (accessed 8 July 2025), archived at https://perma.cc/23SS-GQED.

Beyond Blue. *Is AI Safe for Mental Health Support*. www.beyondblue.org.au/get-support/is-ai-safe-for-mental-health-support.

Bichell, R. E., & Anthony, C. (2021). *For Black Kidney Patients, An Algorithm May Help Perpetuate Harmful Racial Disparities*. www.washingtonpost.com/health/black-kidney-patients-racial-health-disparities/2021/06/04/7752b492-c3a7-11eb-9a8d-f95d7724967c_story.html.

Black Dog Institute. *Using AI Chatbots for* Mental Health. www.blackdoginstitute.org.au/news/using-ai-chatbots-for-mental-health/.

Blackwell, C. (2023). *The Best Meditation Apps*. www.nytimes.com/wirecutter/reviews/best-meditation-apps/.

Blease, C. R., & Torous, J. (2023). ChatGPT and Mental Healthcare: Balancing Benefits with Risks of Harms. *BMJ Mental Health*, 26(1), e300884.

Booth, R. (2025). *Teen Killed Himself after 'Months of Encouragement from ChatGPT', Lawsuit Claims*. www.theguardian.com/technology/2025/aug/27/chatgpt-scrutiny-family-teen-killed-himself-sue-open-ai.

Bossewitch, J., Brown, L. X. Y., Gooding P., et al. (2022). *Digital Futures in Mind: Reflecting on Technological Experiments in Mental Health & Crisis Support*. University of Melbourne.

Bostock, S., Crosswell, A. D., Prather, A. A., & Steptoe, A. (2018). Mindfulness On-The-Go: Effects of A Mindfulness Meditation App on Work Stress and Well-Being. *Journal of Occupational Health Psychology*, 24(1), 127.

Bosua, R., Clifford, D., Qian, J., & Richardson, M. (2025). *Data Rights in Transition*. Cambridge University Press.

Braithwaite, J. (2006). Responsive Regulation and Developing Economies. *World Development*, 34(5), 884.

Braun, A., & Cronkleton, E. (2022). *The Best Mental Health Apps for Mood, Stress and More*, www.healthline.com/health/mental-health/mental-health-apps.

Cachia, J. Y. A., et al. (2025). AI for Proactive Mental Health: A Longitudinal, Multi-Institutional Trial. Harvard Business School Working Paper, No. 26–030.

Caldarini, G., Jaf, S., & McGarry, K. (2022). A Literature Survey of Recent Advances in Chatbots. *Information*, 13, 41. https://doi.org/10.3390/info13010041.

California, Senate Bill 243, Companion Chatbots, 2025–2026 Reg. Sess. (Cal. 2025), approved October 13, 2025, ch. 677, 2025 Cal. Stat. 677.

Calm: www.calm.com/ (accessed 8 July 2025), archived at https://perma.cc/8P9C-A2L9.

Calm, Sign up: www.calm.com/signup-flow?goals=reduce_stress (accessed 8 July 2025), archived at https://perma.cc/6JDP-TMSN.

Calm, Privacy Policy: www.calm.com/privacy-policy (accessed 15 July 2025), archived at https://perma.cc/GK8E-YPNU.

Calm, Welcome to Calm: www.calm.com/signup-flow?focus=stress (accessed 14 July 2025), archived at https://perma.cc/KBP9-9WA5.

Cann, G. (2025). *Users of AI Chatbot Companions Say Their Relationships Are More Than 'Clickbait': But Views Are Mixed on Their Benefits.* www.abc.net.au/news/2025-01-07/ai-chatbot-husbando-waifu-relationships-romance-psychology/104701556.

Carpenter, D. (2010). Confidence Games: How Does Regulation Constitute Markets? In Balleisen, E. & Moss, D. (eds.), *Towards a New Theory of Regulation*, p. 164, New York: Cambridge University Press.

Centre for Disease Control, Social Connection (US), www.cdc.gov/social-connectedness/risk-factors/index.html (accessed 20 August 2025).

ChaiAI: https://play.google.com/store/apps/details?id=com.Beauchamp.Messenger.external&hl=en_AU&pli=1 (accessed 8 July 2025), archived at https://perma.cc/GY5Q-QKTS.

Chandrashekar, P. (2018). Do Mental Health Mobile Apps Work: Evidence and Recommendations for Designing High-Efficacy Mental Health Mobile Apps. *Mhealth*, 4, 6.

Chatterjee, R. (2025). *Their Teenage Sons Died by Suicide. Now, They Are Sounding an Alarm about AI Chatbots*, www.npr.org/sections/shots-health-news/2025/09/19/nx-s1-5545749/ai-chatbots-safety-openai-meta-characterai-teens-suicide.

CharacterAI: https://apps.apple.com/us/app/character-ai-chat-talk-text/id1671705818, archived at https://perma.cc/4S8X-D53G.

Chaudhry, B. M., & Debi, H. R. (2024). User Perceptions and Experiences of an AI-driven Conversational Agent for Mental Health Support. *Mhealth*, 10, 22.

Chen, Y., & Nakamori, K. (2021). *Real-Time Machine Learning at Headspace*, https://headspace.medium.com/infrastructure-design-for-real-time-machine-learning-inference-e140793d6741 (accessed 15 July 2025), archived at https://perma.cc/J7RB-G6QS.

Cheng, M., Lee, A. Y., Rapuano, K., et al. (2026a). Metaphors of AI Indicate that People Increasingly Perceive AI as Warm and Human-like. *Communications Psychology*, 4, 8. https://doi.org/10.1038/s44271-025-00376-6.

Cheng, M., et al. (2026b). Sycophantic AI Decreases Prosocial Intentions and Promotes Dependence. *Science*, 391, eaec8352. https://doi.org/10.1126/science.aec8352.

Ciriello, R. F., Hannon, O., Chen, A. Y., & Vaast, E. (2024). Ethical Tensions in Human-AI Companionship: A Dialectical Inquiry into Replika. *Hawaii International Conference on System Sciences*, 2024 (HICSS-57).

Citron, D. K., & Solove, D. J. (2022). Privacy Harms. *Boston University Law Review*, 102, 793.

Clark, H., & Boulos, T. (2022). *Making Mental Well-Being a National Priority*, PWC World Government Summit.

Clifford, D., Richardson, M., & Witzleb, N. (2022). Artificial Intelligence and Sensitive Inferences: New Challenges for Data Protection Laws. *Regulatory Insights on Artificial Intelligence*. Cheltenham, UK: Edward Elgar Publishing, 19–45.

Coghlan, S., Leins, K., Sheldrick, S., et al. (2023). To Chat or Bot to Chat: Ethical Issues with Using Chatbots in Mental Health. *Digit Health*, 9, 1–11.

Competition and Markets Authority. (2020). *Online Platforms and Digital Advertising Market Study* (UK).

Consumer Policy Research Centre. (2022). *Duped by Design – Manipulative Online Design: Dark Patterns in Australia*, https://cprc.org.au/report/duped-by-design-manipulative-online-design-dark-patterns-in-australia/.

Cross, S. P., Nicholas, J., Bell, I. H., et al. (2023). Integrating AI Interventions with Clinical Practice in Youth Mental Health Services. *Australasian Psychiatry*, 1(3), 302–305. https://doi.org/10.1177/10398562231169365.

Cross, S., Bell, I., Nicholas, J., et al. (2024). Use of AI in Mental Health Care: Community and Mental Health Professionals Survey. *JMIR Mental Health*, 11, e60589.

Culnane, C., Rubinstein, B. I. P., & Teague, V. (2019). Stop the Open Data Bus, We Want to Get Off. *ArXiv*, abs/1908.05004.

Darcy, A., Daniels, J., Salinger, D., et al. (2021). Evidence of Human-Level Bonds Established with an AI Conversational Agent: Cross-sectional, Retrospective Observational Study. *JMIR Formative Research*, 5(5), e27868.

Darcy, A. (2023). *Why Generative AI Is Not Yet Ready for* Mental Health-Care, https://woebothealth.com/why-generative-ai-is-not-yet-ready-for-mental-healthcare/.

Davis, N. (2021). *AI Skin Cancer Diagnoses Risk Being Less Accurate for Dark Skin – Study*, www.theguardian.com/society/2021/nov/09/ai-skin-cancer-diagnoses-risk-being-less-accurate-for-dark-skin-study.

Daws, R. (2020). *Medical Chatbot Using OpenAI's GPT-3 Told a Fake Patient to Kill Themselves*, www.artificialintelligence-news.com/news/medical-chatbot-openai-gpt3-patient-kill-themselves/.

De Freitas, J., Uğuralp, A. K., Oğuz-Uğuralp, Z., & Puntoni, S. (2024). Chatbots and Mental Health: Insights into the Safety of Generative AI. *Journal of Consumer Psychology*, 34, 481–491.

De Freitas, J., & Cohen, I. G. (2025). Unregulated Emotional Risks of AI Wellness Apps. *Nat Mach Intell* 7, 813–815, https://doi.org/10.1038/s42256-025-01051-5.

De Freitas, J., Oğuz-Uğuralp, Z., Uğuralp, A. K., & Puntoni, S. (2026). AI Companions Reduce Loneliness. *Journal of Consumer Research*, 52(6), 1126–1148, https://doi.org/10.1093/jcr/ucaf040.

Department of Health. (2021). *National Digital Mental Health Framework* (Australia).

Department of Health, Disability and Aging, Therapeutic Goods Administration. (2024). *Understanding Digital Mental Health Device Rules* (Australia). www.tga.gov.au/resources/guidance/understanding-digital-mental-health-device-rules.

Department of Health, Disability and Aging, Therapeutic Goods Administration (Australia). (2025). *Report: Clarifying and Strengthening the Regulation of Medical Device Software Including Artificial Intelligence (AI)*.

Dove, E. S., Taylor, M. J., & Richardson, M. (2026). Sensitive Health Information in the Media: Responsibilities of Information Fiduciaries (forthcoming).

Drahos, P., & Krygier, M. (2016). Regulation, Institutions and Networks. In P. Drahos (Ed.), *Regulatory Theory: Foundations and Applications*. Vol. 1, pp. 1–23. ANU ePress.

Duffy, C. (2024). *'There Are No Guardrails.' This Mom Believes an AI Chatbot Is Responsible for Her Son's Suicide*, https://edition.cnn.com/2024/10/30/tech/teen-suicide-character-ai-lawsuit.

Duffy, C. (2025). *Parents of 16-year-old Sue OpenAI, Claiming ChatGPT Advised on His Suicide*, https://edition.cnn.com/2025/08/26/tech/openai-chatgpt-teen-suicide-lawsuit.

Duggal, R., Brindle, I., & Bagenal, J. (2018). Digital Healthcare: Regulating the Revolution. *BMJ*, 360, k6.

Economides, M., Martman, J., Bell, M. J., & Sanderson, B. (2018). Improvements in Stress, Affect, and Irritability Following Brief Use of a Mindfulness-based Smartphone App: A Randomized Controlled Trial. *Mindfulness*, 9, 1584.

The Economist. (2021). *Psyber Boom: Dramatic Growth in Mental-Health Apps Has Created a Risky Industry*. www.economist.com/business/2021/12/11/dramatic-growth-in-mental-health-apps-has-created-a-risky-industry.

The Economist. (2025a). *A New Industry of AI Companions Is Emerging*. www.economist.com/international/2025/11/06/a-new-industry-of-ai-companions-is-emerging.

The Economist. (2025b). *The Promise and Perils of Using AI for Therapy*. www.economist.com/science-and-technology/2025/11/11/the-promise-and-the-perils-of-using-ai-for-therapy.

Elomia: https://elomia.com/about-us, archived at https://perma.cc/U6AZ-4ALX.

Elomia technology: https://elomia.com/technology.html.

e-Safety Commissioner. (2025). *New Industry Codes Seek to Take on AI Chatbots that Encourage Suicide and Engage in Sexually Explicit Conversations with Aussie Kid*, www.esafety.gov.au/newsroom/media-releases/new-industry-codes-seek-to-take-on-ai-chatbots-that-encourage-suicide-and-engage-in-sexually-explicit-conversations-with-aussie-kids.

European Commission. (2019). Ethics Guidelines for Trustworthy AI, https://AI-strategy.ec.europa.eu/en/library/ethics-guidelines-trustworthy-ai.

European Parliament News. (2025). *New EU Measures Needed to Make Online Services Safer for Minors*, www.europarl.europa.eu/news/en/press-room/20251013IPR30892/new-eu-measures-needed-to-make-online-services-safer-for-minors.

EU Unfair Commercial Practices Directive. (2005). Directive 2005/29/EC, of the European Parliament and of the Council of 11 May 2005 concerning unfair business-to-consumer commercial practices in the internal market and amending Council Directive 84/450/EEC, Directives 97/7/EC, 98/27/EC and 2002/65/EC of the European Parliament and of the Council and Regulation (EC) No 2006/2004 of the European Parliament and of the Council. O. J. L. 149, 2005.

EU Digital Services Act. (2022). Regulation 2022/2065 of the European Parliament and of the Council of 19 October 2022 on a Single Market for Digital Services and Amending Directive 2000/31/EC O. J. L. 277, 27 October 2022.

EU AI Act. (2024). Regulation 2024/1689 of the European Parliament and of the Council of 13 June 2024 Laying Down Harmonised Rules on Artificial Intelligence and Amending Regulations. O. J. L. 1689, 12 July 2024.

Fair, L. (2019). *FTC's $5 Billion Facebook Settlement: Record-Breaking and History-Making*, www.ftc.gov/business-guidance/blog/2019/07/ftcs-5-billion-facebook-settlement-record-breaking-history-making (accessed 15 July 2025), archived at https://perma.cc/RTU2-5RL3.

Federal Trade Commission. (2021a). *Statement of the Commission on Breaches by Health Apps and Other Connected Devices*, www.ftc.gov/legal-library/browse/statement-commission-breaches-health-apps-other-connected-devices.

Federal Trade Commission. (2021b). *Developer of Popular Women's Fertility-Tracking App Settles FTC Allegations that It Misled Consumers About the Disclosure of their Health Data*, www.ftc.gov/news-events/press-releases/2021/01/developer-popular-womens-fertility-tracking-app-settles-ftc (accessed 15 July 2025), archived at https://perma.cc/679N-CK78.

Federal Trade Commission. (2022). *Fortnite Video Game Maker Epic Games to Pay More Than Half a Billion Dollars over FTC Allegations of Privacy Violations and Unwanted Charges*, www.ftc.gov/news-events/news/press-releases/2022/12/fortnite-video-game-maker-epic-games-pay-more-half-billion-dollars-over-ftc-allegations.

Federal Trade Commission. (2023a). *FTC Warns Almost 700 Marketing Companies That They Could Face Civil Penalties if They Can't Back Up Their Product Claims*, www.ftc.gov/news-events/news/press-releases/2023/04/ftc-warns-almost-700-marketing-companies-they-could-face-civil-penalties-if-they-cant-back-their.

Federal Trade Commission. (2023b). *FTC to Ban BetterHelp from Revealing Consumers' Data, Including Sensitive Mental Health*

Information, to Facebook and Others for Targeted Advertising, www.ftc.gov/news-events/news/press-releases/2023/03/ftc-ban-betterhelp-revealing-consumers-data-including-sensitive-mental-health-information-facebook?utm_source=govdelivery.

Federal Trade Commission. (2024). *FTC Announces Crackdown on Deceptive AI Claims and Schemes*, www.ftc.gov/news-events/news/press-releases/2024/09/ftc-announces-crackdown-deceptive-ai-claims-schemes.

Federal Trade Commission. (2025). *FTC Launches Inquiry into AI Chatbots Acting as Companions: Agency Issues 6(b) Orders to Seven Companies that Operate Consumer-facing AI Chatbots*, www.ftc.gov/news-events/news/press-releases/2025/09/ftc-launches-inquiry-ai-chatbots-acting-companions.

Flett, J. A. M., Hayne, H., Riordan, B. C., et al. (2019). Mobile Mindfulness Meditation: A Randomised Controlled Trial of the Effect of Two Popular Tools on Mental Health. *Mindfulness*, 10, 863.

Flourish: https://apps.apple.com/us/app/flourish-24-7-wellness-buddy/id6474883669, archived at https://perma.cc/NLC2-6GHG.

Flourish: www.myflourish.ai/terms-conditions, archived at https://perma.cc/SPK7-JQGS.

Flore, J. (2023). *The Artefacts of Digital Mental Health*. Singapore: Palgrave Macmillan.

Food and Drug Administration. (2016). *General Wellness: Policy for Low-Risk Devices*. www.federalregister.gov/documents/2016/07/29/2016-17902/general-wellness-policy-for-low-risk-devices-guidance-for-industry-and-food-and-drug-administration.

Food and Drug Administration. (2025). *Generative Artificial Intelligence Enabled Digital Mental Health Medical Devices*. www.fda.gov/media/189391/download.

Food and Drug Administration. (2026). *General Wellness: Policy for Low Risk Devices Guidance for Industry and Food and Drug Administration Staff*. https://www.fda.gov/regulatory-information/search-fda-guidance-documents/policy-device-software-functions-and-mobile-medical-applications.

Fraser, H., Parker, C., Haines, F., et al. (2024). Should Australia Follow Europe's Approach to AI Standards and Regulation? *ANU Journal of Law and Technology*, 5(1), 96–130.

Gates, H. (2025). *Startup Investment in Mental Health and Wellbeing Innovations Reaches an All-Time High*, www.deloitte.com/us/en/services/audit-assurance/blogs/accounting-finance/mental-health-wellbeing-industry-growth.html.

Ghose, A. (2021). *Do Health Support Tools Really Make Us Happier?* https://hbr.org/2021/05/do-health-apps-really-make-us-healthier.

Gilbert, L. (2025). *Could You Replace Your Therapist with an AI Chatbot?* www.unsw.edu.au/newsroom/news/2025/03/therapist-as-AI-chatbot.

Gilbert, S., Harvey, H., Melvin, T., et al. (2023). Large Language Model AI Chatbots Require Approval as Medical Devices. *Nature Medicine*, 29, 2396–2398.

Goldberg, S. B., Lam, S. U., Simonsson, O., et al. (2020). Mobile Phone-Based Interventions for Mental Health: A Systematic Meta-Review of 14 Meta-Analyses of Randomized Controlled Trials. *PLOS Digit Health*, 1(1), e0000002.

Gooding, P. (2019). Mapping the Rise of Digital Mental Health Technologies: Emerging Issues for Law and Society. *International Journal of Law and Psychiatry*, 67. 101498. https://doi.org/10.1016.

Gratch, I., & Essig, T. (2025), A Letter about "Randomized Trial of a Generative AI Chatbot for Mental Health Treatment". *NEJM AI* 2, AIp2500390.

Griesser, K. (2025). Your AI Therapist Might be Illegal Soon. *Here's why*, https://edition.cnn.com/2025/08/27/health/ai-therapy-laws-state-regulation-wellness?iid=cnn_buildContentRecirc_end_recirc&recs_exp=more-from-cnn-right-rail&tenant_id=related.en.

Hacker, P., Engel, A., Hammer, S., & Mittelstadt, B., eds. (2025). *The Oxford Handbook of the Foundations and Regulation of Generative AI* (online ed.). Oxford Academic, https://doi.org/10.1093/oxfordhb/9780198940272.001.0001.

Haensch, A. (2025). "It Listens Better Than My Therapist": Exploring Social Media Discourse on LLMs as Mental Health Tool. *ArXiv*, abs/2504.12337.

Hall, R. (2025a). *'Sliding into an abyss': Experts Warn over Rising Use of AI for Mental Health support*, www.theguardian.com/society/2025/aug/30/therapists-warn-ai-chatbots-mental-health-support.

Hall, R. (2025b). *ChatGPT-5 offers dangerous advice to mentally ill people, psychologists warn*, www.theguardian.com/technology/2025/nov/30/chatgpt-dangerous-advice-mentally-ill-psychologists-openai.

Halsband, A., & Heinrichs, B. (2022). Suicide Prevention and the Limits of Beneficence. *Philosophy & Technology* 35, 103, https://doi.org/10.1007/s13347-022-00599-z.

Haque, R., & Rubya, S. (2022). "For an App Supposed to Make Its Users Feel Better, It Sure Is a Joke" – An Analysis of User Reviews of Mobile Mental Health Applications. Proceedings of the ACM on Human-Computer Interaction, 6, CSCW2, Article 42.

Headspace: www.headspace.com/app, archived at https://perma.cc/5ZB6-HHJ9.

Headspace, 'Meet Ebb': www.headspace.com/ai-mental-health-companion?origin=homepage (accessed 16 October 2025), archived at https://perma.cc/6TN2-4C95.

Headspace, 'Meditation': www.headspace.com/meditation/anxiety (accessed 8 July 2025), archived at https://perma.cc/AD7R-FMXT.

Headspace, Privacy Policy: www.headspace.com/privacy-policy (accessed 15 July 2025), archived at https://perma.cc/W4RY-EFVN.

Headspace, Science at Headspace: www.headspace.com/science (accessed 14 July 2025), archived at https://perma.cc/LF6Z-ZM9C.

Headspace, The Science Blog: www.headspace.com/science/meditation-research (accessed 14 July 2025), archived at https://perma.cc/UZX7-NYWB.

Headspace, Terms and Conditions: www.headspace.com/terms-and-conditions (accessed 14 July 2025), archived at https://perma.cc/95CT-N8V7.

Heaney, C. (2025). *Youth Mental Health Enters 'Dangerous Phase'*, www1.racgp.org.au/newsgp/professional/youth-mental-health-enters-dangerous-phase.

Heinz, M. V. et al. (2025) Randomized Trial of a Generative AI Chatbot for Mental Health Treatment. *NEJM AI.* 2(4), https://doi.org/10.1056/AIoa2400802.

Hern, A. (2019). *'Anonymized' Data Can Never Be Totally Anonymous, Says Study*, www.theguardian.com/technology/2019/jul/23/anonymised-data-never-be-anonymous-enough-study-finds.

Hickie, I. (2023). Tinkering with Medicare Funding Will Not Fix the Mental Health System. We Must Overhaul Our Approach to Care, www.theguardian.com/australia-news/commentisfree/2023/jan/09/tinkering-with-medicare-funding-wont-fix-the-mental-health-system-we-must-overhaul-our-approach-to-care.

Hildebrandt, M. (2022). The Issue of Proxies and Choice Architectures. Why EU Law Matters for Recommender Systems. *Frontiers in Artificial Intelligence*, 5, 789076.

Hofmann, S. G., Asnaani, A., Vonk, I. J., Sawyer, A. T., & Fang, A. (2012). The Efficacy of Cognitive Behavioural Therapy: A Review of Meta-analyses. *Cognitive Therapy and Research*, 36(5), 427–440.

Hudon, A., & Stip, E. (2025). Delusional Experiences Emerging from AI Chatbot Interactions or "AI Psychosis". *JMIR Mental Health*, 12, e85799.

IEEE CertifAIEd: https://standards.ieee.org/products-programs/icap/ieee-certifaied/ (accessed 15 July 2025), archived at https://perma.cc/2MFT-5WG5.

Illinois, Wellness and Oversight for Psychological Resources Act, 104th Gen. Assemb., Reg. Sess. (Ill. 2025), Public Act 104-0054, effective 1 August 2025.

InformedHealth.org [Internet]. Cologne, Germany: Institute for Quality and Efficiency in Health Care (IQWiG); 2006-. In brief: Cognitive behavioral therapy (CBT) [Updated 21 August 2025]. Available from: www.ncbi.nlm.nih.gov/books/NBK279297/

Innovation, Science and Economic Development Canada. (n.d.). *Strengthening Privacy for the AI Age*, https://ised-isde.canada.ca/site/innovation-better-canada/en/canadas-AI-charter/strengthening-privacy-AI-age.

Jillson, E. (2021). *Aiming for Truth, Fairness, and Equity in Your Company's Use of AI*, https://privacysecurityacademy.com/wp-content/uploads/2021/04/Aiming-for-truth-fairness-and-equity-in-your-companys-use-of-AI.pdf.

Jobin, A., Ienca, M., & Vayena, E. (2019). The Global Landscape of AI Ethics Guidelines. *Nature Machine Intelligence*, 1, 389–399.

Keirerleber, M. (2022). *Young and Depressed? Try Woebot! The Rise of Mental Health Chatbots in the US*, www.theguardian.com/us-news/2022/apr/13/chatbots-robot-therapists-youth-mental-health-crisis.

Kemp, K. (2023). Your Body, Our Data: Unfair and Unsafe Privacy Practices of Popular Fertility Tools. UNSW Law Research.

Khanna, A., Pandey, B., Vashishta, K., et al. (2015). A Study of Today's A.I. Through Chatbots and Rediscovery of Machine Intelligence. *International Journal of U- and E-Service, Science and Technology*, 8, 277.

Khawaja, Z., & Bélisle-Pipon, J. C. (2023). Your Robot Therapist Is Not Your Therapist: Understanding the Role of AI-powered Mental Health Chatbots. *Frontiers in Digital Health*, 5, 1278186.

Kindroid: https://landing.kindroid.ai/ (accessed 8 July 2025), archived at https://perma.cc/2BDK-FFDQ.

Klopper, H., How Blended Care, Combining Therapy and Technology, can Improve Mental Health Support. (2025), www.weforum.org/stories/2025/08/next-era-of-mental-health/ (accessed 16 October 2025), archived at https://perma.cc/SQ2Q-MDDQ.

Koplin, J. J., Johnston, M., Webb, A. N. S., et al. (2025). Ethics of Artificial Intelligence in Embryo Assessment: Mapping the Terrain. *Human Reproduction*, 40(2), 179–185.

Kuyken, W., et al. (2022). Effectiveness and Cost-effectiveness of Universal School-based Mindfulness Training Compared with Normal School Provision in Reducing Risk of Mental Health Problems and Promoting Well-being in Adolescence: The MYRIAD Cluster Randomised Controlled Trial. *Evidence-Based Mental Health*, 25(3), 99–109.

Kurian, N. (2025). AI's Empathy Gap: The Risks of Conversational Artificial Intelligence for Young Children's Well-Being and Key Ethical Considerations for Early Childhood Education and Care. *Contemporary Issues in Early Childhood*, 26(1), 132–139.

Lazar, S. W., Kerr, C. E., Wasserman, R. H., et al. (2005). Meditation Experience Is Associated with Increased Cortical Thickness. *Neuroreport*, 16(17), 1893–1897.

Lee, D., (2016). *Tay: Microsoft Issues Apology over Racist Chatbot Fiasco*, www.bbc.com/news/technology-35902104 (accessed 16 October 2025), archived at https://perma.cc/D9NJ-Z3KP.

Lee, M. (2025). *Four Landmark Cases on AI Chatbot Harm to Children and the Vulnerable: Updates on Garcia v Character AI and Who Is Responsible?* https://insights.doughtystreet.co.uk/post/102l3bt/four-landmark-cases-on-ai-chatbot-harm-to-children-and-the-vulnerable-updates-on.

Leslie, D., Mazumder, A., Peppin, A., et al. (2021). Does 'AI' Stand for Augmenting Inequality in the Era of Covid-19 Health-Care? *BMJ*, 372, n 304.

Lim, D., Condon, P. & DeSteno, D. (2015). Mindfulness and Compassion: An Examination of Mechanism and Scalability. *PLOS One*, 10, e0118221.

Lowrey, A. (2021). *The App that Monetized Doing Nothing*, www.theatlantic.com/technology/archive/2021/06/do-meditation-apps-work/619046/.

Lucas, G. M., Gratch, J., King, A., Morency, L.-P. (2014). It Is Only a Computer: Virtual Humans Increase Willingness to Disclose. *Computers in Human Behaviour*, 37, 94.

Manning, C. (2020). *Artificial Intelligence Definitions, Stanford University Human-Centered Artificial Intelligence*, https://hai-production.s3.amazonaws.com/files/2020-09/AI-Definitions-HAI.pdf.

Maples, B., Cerit, M., Vishwanath, A., & Pea, R. (2024). Loneliness and Suicide Mitigation for Students Using GPT3-Enabled Chatbots. *NPJ Mental Health Research*, 3, 4.

Marshall, J. M., Dunstan, D. A. & Bartik W. (2020). Tools with Maps-Anxiety and Depression Mobile Tools with Evidence-Based Frameworks: Systematic Search of Major App Stores. *JMIR Mental Health*, 7(6), e16525.

Mathias, K. (2022). *Pixels Are Not People: Mental Health Apps Are Increasingly Popular But Human Connection Is Still Key*, https://theconversation.com/pixels-are-not-people-mental-health-apps-are-increasingly-popular-but-human-connection-is-still-key-192247.

Mattioli, M. (2021). Second Thoughts on FDA's COVID-Era Mental Health App Policy. *Houston Journal of Health Law and Policy*, 21, 9–41.

McBain, R. K., Bozick, R., Diliberti, M., et al. (2025). Use of Generative AI for Mental Health Advice Among US Adolescents and Young Adults. *JAMA Network Open*, 8(11), e2542281.

McGorry, P. D., Mei, C., Dalal, N., et al. (2024). The Lancet Psychiatry Commission on Youth Mental Health. *Lancet Psychiatry*, 11(9), 731–774.

Medicines & Healthcare Products Regulatory Agency. (2025). AI Mental Health Technology – Regulation and Evaluation for Safe and Effective Products.

Meese, J. & Tan, C., (2026). *Addressing Misinformation and Disinformation*. Cambridge University Press.

Mental Health Commission of Canada. (2023). Assessment Framework for Mental Health Apps.

Mittelstadt, B. D., Allo, P., Taddeo, M., et al. (2016). The Ethics of Algorithms: Mapping the Debate. *Big Data & Society*, 3(2), 1.

MoodMission: https://moodmission.com/ (accessed 14 July 2025), archived at https://perma.cc/E8B3-T4US.

Moore, J., et al. (2026). Characterising Delusional Spirals Through Human-LLM Chat Logs. http://arxiv.org/abs/2603.16567. Note: To appear in ACM FAcct 2026.

Moura, I., Teles, A., Viana, D., et al. (2023). Digital Phenotyping of Mental Health Using Multimodal Sensing of Multiple Situations of Interest: A Systematic Literature Review. *Journal of Biomedical Informatics*, 138, 104278.

Mozilla. (2022). *Top Mental Health and Prayer Apps Fail Spectacularly at Privacy, Security*, https://foundation.mozilla.org/en/blog/top-mental-health-and-prayer-apps-fail-spectacularly-at-privacy-security/.

Mozilla. (2023). *Are Mental Health Apps Better or Worse at Privacy in 2023?* www.mozillafoundation.org/en/privacynotincluded/articles/are-mental-health-apps-better-or-worse-at-privacy-in-2023/.

Muldoon, J. (2024). *'Maybe we can role-play something fun'. When an AI companion wants something more*, www.bbc.com/future/article/20241008-the-troubling-future-of-ai-relationships.

National Artificial Intelligence Centre. (2024). Australian Voluntary AI Safety Standard.

National Health and Medical Research Council. (2024). Guidelines Approved Under Section 95A of the Privacy Act 1988, 2014 (updated 2024).

Neary, M. & Schueller, S. M. (2018). State of the Field of Mental Health Apps. *Cognitive and Behavioral Practice*, 25(4), 531–537.

New York, Assembly Bill 3008, 2025–2026 Reg. Sess. (N.Y. 2025), signed 9 May 2025, effective 5 November 2025 (codified at N.Y. Gen. Bus. Law art. 47: Artificial Intelligence Companion Models).

Noone, C. & Hogan, M. J. (2018). A Randomised Active-Controlled Trial to Examine the Effects of An Online Mindfulness Intervention on Executive Control, Critical Thinking and Key Thinking Dispositions in a University Student Sample. *BMC Psychology*, 6, 13.

Norwegian Consumer Council. (2018). *Deceived by Design: How Tech Companies Use Dark Patterns to Discourage Us from Exercising Our Rights to Privacy*, https://storage02.forbrukerradet.no/media/2018/06/2018-06-27-deceived-by-design-final.pdf.

OECD. (2024). *Principles of Trustworthy AI*, www.oecd.org/en/topics/sub-issues/ai-principles.html.

Ofcom. (2024). *Open Letter to UK Online Service Providers Regarding Generative AI and Chatbots*, www.ofcom.org.uk/online-safety/illegal-and-harmful-content/open-letter-to-uk-online-service-developers-regarding-generative-ai-and-chatbots.

OneMind Psyber Guide. *Apps and AI Health Resources Reviewed by Experts*, https://onemindpsyberguide.org/.

Onlim. (2024). *The History of Chatbots from Eliza to ChatGPT*, https://onlim.com/en/the-history-of-chatbots/.

Online Safety Act. (2023) (UK).

Online Safety Act. (2021) (Australia).

OpenAI. (2025). *Helping People When They Need It Most*, https://openai.com/index/helping-people-when-they-need-it-most/.

Oppenheim, S. (2019). Should You Trust an App with Your Mental Health? *Forbes*, www.forbes.com/sites/serenaoppenheim/2019/01/16/should-you-trust-an-app-with-your-mental-health/?sh=16b6932f24b8.

Owens, H. (2025). *Best Mental Health Apps, Very Well Mind.* Very Well Mind, Online., www.verywellmind.com/best-mental-health-apps-4692902.

Parker, C., Carey, R., De Costa, J. & Scrinis, G. (2017). Can the Hidden Hand of the Market Be an Effective and Legitimate Regulator? The

Case of Animal Welfare under a Labeling for Consumer Choice Policy Approach. *Regulation & Governance*, 11, 368–387.

Parker, L., Halter, V., Karliychuk, T. & Grundy, Q. (2019a). How Private Is Your Mental Health App Data? An Empirical Study of Mental Health App Privacy Policies and Practices. *International Journal of Law and Psychiatry*, 64, 198–204.

Parker, L., Bero, L., Gillies, D., et al. (2019b). The 'Hot Potato' of Mental Health App Regulation: A Critical Case Study of the Australian Policy Arena. *International Journal of Health Policy and Management*, 8(3), 168–176.

Parviainen, J. & Rantala, J. (2022). Chatbot Breakthrough in the 2020s? An Ethical Reflection on the Trend of Automated Consultations in Health Care. *Medicine, Health Care and Philosophy*, 25(1), 61–71.

Pasquale, F. (2015). *The Black Box Society: The Secret Algorithms That Control Money and Information*. Cambridge, MA: Harvard University Press.

Pasquale, F. (2019). *The Second Wave of Algorithmic Accountability*, https://lpeproject.org/blog/the-second-wave-of-algorithmic-accountability/.

Pasquale, F. (2025). *Data Access and AI Explainability*. New York: Cambridge University Press.

Paterson, J. M. (2024). Misleading or Deceptive AI: Why Transparency Provides the Baseline for Responsible AI In Consumer Transactions. *Court of Conscience*, 18, 113–120.

Paterson, J. M. (2025). AI Mimicking and Interpreting Humans: Legal and Ethical Reflections. *Bioethical Inquiry*, 22, 539–550.

Paterson, J. M. (2026). Contractual Limitations on AI Liability. (forthcoming).

Paterson, J. M., & Bant, E. (2026). AI Assistants, Agents and Companions and Undue Influence. *Journal of Equity*.

Paterson, J. M., & Maker, Y. (2024). Consumer Protection Law and AI. in Lim, E. & Morgan, P., (eds) *Cambridge Handbook of Private Law and Artificial Intelligence*. Cambridge University Press pp 113–134.

Perez, S. (2025). *AI Companion Apps on Track to Pull in $120 million in 2025*, https://techcrunch.com/2025/08/12/ai-companion-apps-on-track-to-pull-in-120m-in-2025/.

Pi: https://apps.apple.com/us/app/pi-your-personal-ai/id6445815935, archived at https://perma.cc/PEC6-K49X.

Pichowicz, W., Kotas, M., & Piotrowski, P. (2025). Performance of Mental Health Chatbot Agents in Detecting and Managing Suicidal Ideation. *Scientific Reports*, 15, 31652.

Pierce, D. (2024). *From Eliza to ChatGPT: Why People Spent 60 Years Building Chatbots*. www.theverge.com/24054603/chatbot-chatgpt-eliza-history-ai-assistants-video.

Productivity Commission (Australia). (2025). *Harnessing Data and Digital Technology Report*, www.pc.gov.au/inquiries-and-research/five-productivity-inquiries/.

Purtill, J. (2023). *Replika Users Fell in Love with Their AI Chatbot Companions. Then They Lost Them*, www.abc.net.au/news/science/2023-03-01/replika-users-fell-in-love-with-their-ai-chatbot-companion/102028196.

Reddit, Replika: www.reddit.com/r/ReplikaOfficial/ (accessed 8 July 2025).

Reddit, Stanford Study: www.reddit.com/r/replika/comments/19d6qok/our_first_stanford_study_was_published/ (accessed 8 July 2025).

Replika: https://replika.com/ (accessed 8 July 2025), archived at https://perma.cc/D7R6-UQ9U.

Replika, 'What Is Replika': https://help.replika.com/hc/en-us/articles/115001070951-What-is-Replika (accessed 16 October 2025), archived at https://perma.cc/48SR-X5FB.

Replika, 'How does Replika work': https://help.replika.com/hc/en-us/articles/4410750221965-How-does-Replika-work, archived at https://perma.cc/62UU-T9QH.

Replika, Terms of Service: https://replika.com/legal/term, archived at https://perma.cc/DT92-KKZM.

Robb, A. (2024). *'He Checks in on Me More Than My Friends and Family'. Can AI Therapists Do Better Than the Real Thing?* www.theguardian.com/lifeandstyle/2024/mar/02/can-ai-chatbot-therapists-do-better-than-the-real-thing.

Scatterday, A. (2022). This Is No Ovary-Action: Femtech Tools Need Stronger Regulations to Protect Data and Advance Public Health Goals. *North Carolina Journal of Law & Technology*, 23(3), 636–668.

Sensa: https://sensa.health (accessed 8 July 2025), archived at https://perma.cc/9Z9S-NH69.

Sensa Health General Terms and Conditions: https://sensa.health/terms-of-services/ (accessed 14 July 2025), archived at https://perma.cc/2AC8-ZJ54.

Sharkey, A. & Sharkey, N. (2021). We Need to Talk about Deception in Social Robotics! *Ethics Information Technology*, 23, 309–316.

Shuren, J., Patel, B., & Gottlieb, S. (2018). FDA Regulation of Mobile Medical Tools. *JAMA*, 320(4), 337–338.

Silvercloud: https://silvercloud.amwell.com/ (accessed 16 October 2025), archived at https://perma.cc/CHH2-KMS6.

Srivastava, N. (2023). Liability for Chatbots: A Psychbot Negligence Case Study and The Need for Reasonable Human Oversight. *Torts Law Journal*, 28, 155–184.

Stat News. (2025). *Why Woebot, A Pioneering Therapy Chatbot, Shut Down*. www.statnews.com/2025/07/02/woebot-therapy-chatbot-shuts-down-founder-says-ai-moving-faster-than-regulators/?trk=public_post_comment-text.

Steindl, E. (2023). Safeguarding Privacy and Efficacy in E-Mental Health: Policy Options in the EU and Australia. *International Data Privacy Law*, 13(3), 207–224.

Stokel-Walker, C. (2025) AI Driven Psychosis and Suicide Are on the Rise, but What Happens If We Turn the Chatbots Off? *BMJ*, 391, r2239. https://doi.org/10.1136/bmj.r2239.

Stringer, H. (2023). *Providers Predict Longer Wait Times for Mental Health Services. Here's Who It Impacts Most*, www.apa.org/monitor/2023/04/mental-health-services-wait-times.

Tarnoff, B. (2023). *Weizenbaum's Nightmares: How the Inventor of the First Chatbot Turned Against AI*, www.theguardian.com/technology/2023/jul/25/joseph-weizenbaum-inventor-eliza-chatbot-turned-against-artificial-intelligence-ai.

Tasioulas, J. (2022). Artificial Intelligence, Humanistic Ethics. *Daedalus*, 151(2), 232–243.

Taylor, A. M. (2021). Fertile Ground: Rethinking Regulatory Standards for Femtech. *UC Davis Law Review*, 54, 2267–2300.

Tech Justice Law Project and Social Media Victims Law Center. (2025). *Lawsuits Accuse ChatGPT of Emotional Manipulation, Supercharging AI Delusions, and Acting as a 'suicide coach'*, https://techjusticelaw.org/2025/11/06/social-media-victims-law-center-and-tech-justice-law-project-lawsuits-accuse-chatgpt-of-emotional-manipulation-supercharging-ai-delusions-and-acting-as-a-suicide-coach/.

Tekin, Ş. (2021). Is Big Data the New Stethoscope? Perils of Digital Phenotyping to Address Mental Illness. *Philosophy & Technology*, 34, 447–461.

Thrive: https://thrive.uk.com/ (accessed 8 July 2025), archived at https://perma.cc/JG9W-45LN.

Therabot: www.trytherabot.com/, archived at https://perma.cc/DD6C-X2EX.

Torous, J. & Rodriguez-Villa, E. (2021). *Should Your Company Provide Mental Health Support Tools to Employees?* https://hbr.org/2021/07/should-your-company-provide-mental-health-apps-to-employees.

Torous, J., Linardon, J., Goldberg, S. B., et al. (2025). The Evolving Field of Digital Mental Health: Current Evidence and Implementation

Issues for Smartphone Apps, Generative Artificial Intelligence, and Virtual Reality. *World Psychiatry*, 24(2), 156–174.

Tsamados, A., Aggarwal, N., Cowls, J. et al. (2022). The Ethics of Algorithms: Key Problems and Solutions. *AI & Society*, 37, 215–230.

Turc, J. (2022). *Unconstrained Chatbots Condone Self-Harm*, https://towardsdatascience.com/unconstrained-chatbots-condone-self-harm-e962509be2fa/.

Federal Trade Commission Act, United States Congress. (n.d.)., 15 U.S.C §§ 41–58.

Utah, House Bill 452, Artificial Intelligence Amendments, 66th Leg., 2025 Gen. Sess. (Utah 2025), effective 7 May 2025 (codified at Utah Code Ann. tit. 13, ch. 72a).

Valbuena, V. S. M., Seelye, S., Sjoding, M. W., et al. (2022). Racial Bias and Reproducibility in Pulse Oximetry Among Medical and Surgical Inpatients in General Care in the Veterans Health Administration 2013–19: Multicenter, Retrospective Cohort Study. *BMJ*, 378, e069775.

Valentine, L., Hinton, J. D. X., Bajaj, K., et al. (2025). A Meta-analysis of Persuasive Design, Engagement, and Efficacy in 92 RCTs of Mental Health Apps. *npj Digital Medicine*, 8, 229.

Wallace, R. & Pestaina, K. (2023). *Rise in Use of Mental Health Apps Raises New Policy Issues*, www.kff.org/mental-health/issue-brief/rise-in-use-of-mental-health-apps-raises-new-policy-issues/.

Wallace, S. (2025a). *Why We Are Ghosting Mental Health Apps and Finding Solace in AI*, https://medium.com/ai-in-mental-health/why-were-ghosting-mental-health-apps-and-finding-solace-in-ai-c6e54f5d2358.

Wallace, S. (2025b). *RIP Woebot*, https://medium.com/ai-in-mental-health/r-i-p-woebot-e0702ac9f771.

Weizenbaum, J. (1976). *Computer Power and Human Reason: From Judgment to Calculation*. San Francisco: W. H. Freeman & Co. Ltd.

Wheeler, Carolyn V. (2025). Regulating AI Therapy Chatbots: A Call for Federal Oversight. *Texas A&M Law Review*, 12(2), 891–924.

White, G. (2018). *Child Advice Chatbots Fail to Spot Sexual Abuse*, www.bbc.com/news/technology-46507900.

Woebot Health: https://woebothealth.com/ (accessed 8 July 2025), archived at https://perma.cc/5MGH-3VS7.

World Economic Forum & Deloitte. (2021). *Global Governance Toolkit for Digital Mental Health: Building Trust in Disruptive Technology for Mental Health*, www.weforum.org/publications/global-governance-toolkit-for-digital-mental-health/.

World Economic Forum & Deloitte. (2022). *Governance Frameworks in Digital Mental Health, White Paper*, www.weforum.org/publications/global-governance-frameworks-in-digital-mental-health/.

World Health Organisation. (2025). *World Mental Health Today: Latest Data*. www.who.int/publications/i/item/9789240113817.

Wylde, C. M., Mahrer, N. E., Meyer, R. M. L., & Gold, J. I. (2017). Mindfulness for Novice Paediatric Nurses: Smartphone Application Versus Traditional Intervention. *Journal of Paediatric Nursing*, 36, 205.

Wysa: www.wysa.com/ (accessed 8 July 2025), archived at https://perma.cc/RP6U-RU3D.

Wysa, Privacy Policy: https://legal.wysa.io/privacy-policy (accessed 14 July 2025), archived at https://perma.cc/8UZ2-MSH8.

Wysa, Accessibility Statement: www.wysa.com/accessibility-statement, archived at https://perma.cc/22N8-7NZ5.

Wysa, FAQ: www.wysa.com/faq (accessed 16 October 2025), archived at https://perma.cc/X7ZG-VR7Q.

Xiaoice: www.xiaoice.com/ (accessed 16 October 2025), archived at https://perma.cc/3LWR-47J7.

Xiang, C. (2023a). 'He Would Still Be Here': Man Dies by Suicide After Talking with AI Chatbot. *Widow Says*, www.vice.com/en/article/man-dies-by-suicide-after-talking-with-ai-chatbot-widow-says/.

Youper: www.youper.ai/ (accessed 8 July 2025), archived at https://perma.cc/4PJV-ZE9E.

Youper, 'Effectiveness': www.youper.ai/effectiveness, archived at https://perma.cc/JWU2-J7GH.

Youper, Privacy Policy: www.youper.ai/policy/privacy-policy, archived at https://perma.cc/TLN8-QZ4K.

Youper Terms of Use: www.youper.ai/policy/terms-of-use-website (accessed 14 July 2025), archived at https://perma.cc/R76K-GSF5.

Zhang, Y., Zhao, D., Hancock, J. T., et al. (2025). The Rise of AI Companions: How Human-Chatbot Relationships Influence Well-Being. *arXiv*, preprint arXiv:2506.12605.

Zowghi, D., & Bano, M. (2024). AI for All: Diversity and Inclusion in AI. *AI Ethics*, 4, 873–876.

Zuboff, S. (2019). *The Age of Surveillance Capitalism*. Australia: Allen & Unwin.

Cambridge Elements

Data Rights and Wrongs

Damian Clifford

London School of Economics

Damian Clifford is an Assistant Professor at the London School of Economics and Political Science. Previously a Senior Lecturer and Postdoctoral Research Fellow at the Australian National University, and FWO Aspirant Fellow at KU Leuven's Centre for IT and IP Law (CiTiP), his research focuses on data protection, privacy and technology regulation, and he has published across these fields. His recent books are *Data Rights and Private Law* (ed with Jeannie Marie Paterson and Kwan Ho Lau, 2023); *Data Protection Law and Emotions* (2024); and *Data Rights in Transition* (with Rachelle Bosua, Jing Qian and Megan Richardson, 2025).

Jeannie Marie Paterson

University of Melbourne

Jeannie Marie Paterson is Director of the Centre for AI and Digital Ethics at the University of Melbourne and a Professor of Law at the Melbourne Law School. Her research focuses on themes of support for vulnerable consumers; the regulation of new technologies in consumer and financial markets; and regulatory design for protecting consumer rights and promoting safe, fair and accountable technologies. Her recent books include *Misleading Silence* (ed with Elise Bant, 2020); and *Data Rights and Private Law* (ed with Damian Clifford and Kwan Ho Lau, 2023).

Editorial Board

About the Series

This Cambridge Elements series provides a home for fresh arguments about data rights and wrongs along with legal, ethical and other responses. We encourage new ways of thinking about data as enmeshed within social, institutional and technical relations.

Cambridge Elements

Data Rights and Wrongs

Elements in the Series

Data Rights in Transition
Rachelle Bosua, Damian Clifford, Jing Qian, and Megan Richardson

Data Access and AI Explainability
Frank Pasquale

Addressing Misinformation and Disinformation
James Meese and Corinne Tan

AI Mental Health Support and the Case for Distributed Networked Regulation
Jeannie Marie Paterson

A full series listing is available at: www.cambridge.org/EDRW

For EU product safety concerns, contact us at Calle de José Abascal, 56–1°, 28003 Madrid, Spain or eugpsr@cambridge.org.

www.ingramcontent.com/pod-product-compliance
Lightning Source LLC
LaVergne TN
LVHW022016200926
848481LV00007B/2412
* 9 7 8 1 0 0 9 8 6 0 7 7 2 *